"Laura has built a career by hersel[ ] to understand that in order for her [ ] adapt to the moments and times of her life. What makes her even more remarkable is that she never gave up her personal integrity in this most difficult business. **She has absolute love, command and respect for the craft.** She wants that thing that all actor's want. A part. A chance. It is with great respect that I salute her journey knowing that her life has been much more than just the movies. She has stopped her life and dreams multiple times to invest in others' difficulties. Laura's outward beauty could have guaranteed her much more in this business–perhaps even worldwide fame. She could have taken an easier route for her professional pursuits but instead chose to make it about the work and only the work. **She is a role model in that regard and a true leading lady. Enjoy what she has to say and see if you can see yourself in her journey.** She still has some big important parts to play."
Kevin Costner (Academy and Golden Globe Award Winner)

"She's nailed the daily life of an actor in LA about as perfectly detailed as it gets... You can say that Laura is amazingly correct in everything she says and sees, but she makes you hunt for the urgent need to do it which is at the bottom of all."
Richard Dreyfuss (Academy and Golden Globe Award Winner)

"Laura Cayouette knows what she is doing. She can make an indelible character out of a gesture, a prop or the flash of her eye. Backed up by her meticulous research, **she knows what a director wants and what an editor needs to tell the story. She's the real deal.**"
Dennis Christopher (Golden Globe Nominee & BAFTA award winner. *Breaking Away, Django Unchained*)

"Anyone who has met Laura knows that she is unforgettable. Perhaps even more impressive is that she has found a way to translate this personal charisma and life-force into her appearances on screen, making the most of every second of camera time given to her. **She has literally figured out a way to bottle lightning.** I'm sure that her observations and guidance will be invaluable to the actor who is looking to make his or her mark in the film world and to build a career, moment by moment."
Lou Diamond Phillips (Golden Globe Nominee. *Courage Under Fire, La Bamba*)

"Laura has strength, courage and the conviction and, pardon my French but, the balls to hold on to her place in this business. Read her book and you'll find out how."
Joanna Cassidy (Golden Globe Winner, Emmy Nominee. *Six Feet Under*)

"I've worked with Laura as a director and an actress–her easygoing spirit is infectious, and her craft is solid. And after years of experience, she has a lot of practical advice to offer–new actors would do well to listen up!"
Danica McKellar (Actress: *The Wonder Years, The West Wing* and Author: *Math Doesn't Suck*)

"I write off most of these books. But this one I can't. It stands far above most giving smart, logical, realistic and poignant advice. Laura speaks with great intelligence about what must be the most difficult career choice one can make and most importantly how to survive having made that choice."
George W. Perkins (Executive Producer: *Desperate Housewives*, 3-time Emmy Nominee)

"Laura Cayouette is a working actress that also has a happy, well-balanced life. Figuring out how she manages this feat is certainly worth a read."
Reginald Hudlin (Producer: Django Unchained, The Boondocks; Director: Serving Sara, Boomerang)

"**Laura Cayouette's *Know Small Parts* is required reading for everyone with stars in their eyes.** Hollywood is inundated daily with countless dreamers hoping for a career in front of the camera, but no idea how best to pursue one. **Laura's smart, sensible and no nonsense step by step approach to achieving a career as an actor is certain to be the new bible for everyone yearning to break into the biz. I look forward to Laura being thanked in many future Oscar speeches.**"
Adam Rifkin (Writer/Director. Showtime's *Reality Show, Detroit Rock City, Mousehunt*)

"**A must read gift for actors**. Laura Cayouette, a successful actor and renowned journalist **thoroughly lays out a path to artistic fulfillment and success.** Bravo! *The Dude Abides*."
Jeff "The Dude" Dowd (Producer, movie marketing maven *Hoosiers, The Black Stallion, Desperately Seeking Susan)*

"***Know Small Parts* is like having a successful big sister (or big brother) to show you the ropes of Hollywood. Laura's book isn't an academic 'how to' book--its a warm and personal look at how she has actually built a lucrative and fulfilling career.**"
M. Dal Walton, III (Production Executive: *Narc, 16 Blocks, Rambo)*

"Laura Cayouette has created an entire career out of stealing scenes and making moments. *Know Small Parts* boils that down to nuts and bolts information every actor should know."
Scott LaStaiti (Executive Producer: *Love in the Time of Cholera; Runner, Runner*)

"**A clear eyed, detailed, no nonsense guide** to the often mysterious world of TV/Film auditioning and performing. Laura's experience as an actor and producer gives her a 360 view of the process which she shares in the voice of your audition guru; **she's been to the mountain and returned with all the wisdom you'll ever need.**"
Alicia Ruskin (Agency Partner: Kazarian/Spencer/Ruskin & Assoc.)

"**After 30 years in casting....I feel like Laura was sitting on my shoulder all these years. She has expertly explained key notes for an actor to know and understand pursuing their career.** An Actor is in "SHOW" and 'BUSINESS." This book helps the Know How!"
Victoria Burrows (Casting Director: *Lord of the Rings* and *Hobbit* trilogies, *Cast Away*)

"**Any actor would be misguided if they didn't read Laura Cayouette's book. Laura is a first rate actress with solid credentials and knows full well what it takes to succeed in this business.** I would cast her in everything if could!"
Ryan Glorioso, CSA (Casting Director: *Now You See Me, Lay the Favorite*)

"**Whether she's getting laughs or selling sincerity, Laura knows how to turn 30 seconds into something memorable.**"
Mick Dowd (Casting Director: *Revlon, Bud Light, Coke Zero*)

Review by Michael Phillips for the Chicago Tribune

"And in a bit role as a bartender, Laura Cayouette intones the line 'You must be ... The Gent' in a voice so sultry she's halfway to the post-coital cig as she's saying it. Her smile, however, suggests an actual actress having actual fun, in a movie where everyone around her is either hiding behind sunglasses or mud-wrestling."

Review By Linda Stasi for the NY POST

"There are some other interesting females thrown in, such as biker bar owner Dani, played by Laura Cayouette, who steals the show away from, well, everyone."

Know Small Parts

An Actor's Guide to

Turning Minutes into Moments and

Moments into a Career

Laura Cayouette

foreword by:
Richard Dreyfuss

LA to NOLA Press

© 2012 Laura Cayouette

ISBN 978-0-615-72838-4

First Edition: December 2012

Back cover photos by Alain Vasquez, Angela Ellis and James Kong.

The author has made every effort to ensure the accuracy and completeness of information contained in this book. Any slights of people, places, or organizations are unintentional.

For all of the people who supported me along the way,

for the amazing people I met on this journey

and for anyone who ever woke up one day and thought:

I'm supposed to be an actor.

Contents

The Biz

Foreword by Richard Dreyfuss

People say that "it's such a glamorous business." Well it ain't. Well, it is and it isn't. Can be; maybe "mostly not" is better, but even that doesn't cut it. It is what the People who are in it feel it is. It's what they experience for real on a day to day basis and some days, let me tell you, are glorious. Some ain't so.

What Laura has done is given a glimpse of reality–complex, threaded with self-hypnosis, self-denial, and the actuality of real magic slippers–for real people who want, yearn for and see what isn't there and let them know what is there; which sometimes is as as good as it can be, and sometimes makes you see that your soul is really at risk. Both are part of our daily fare in the "biz."

Laura seems to have realized what few ever get to: that one can live a lot of lives in the one life we know we live. She's been up and down. She's been caught by the fever and lived to tell the tale and sees the value in it all without succumbing to the "If I wish it, it will come" that paralyzes so many talented people. She's not saying there's a guarantee or that if you come to be part of it, you'll get chewed up and spit out, she's saying both are part of the life.

If you feel you'll die if you don't try, then for God's sakes get out here and give it a shot. If you want it because your mom wants it, or your mom would disown you if you dared, get another mom. But as our President kind of said a while back, it all depends on what "it" is. If in your head it's all one thing or another, you're wrong. If you know how to appreciate the complex weave of creating dreams while trying to create a dream and you've got the "strong like bull" attitude and the talent and the rigor and the sense of fun within the roller coaster of the whole thing, then you're like Laura–and that's saying a lot.

What is shockingly surprising about what Laura wrote is that as smart as I've known her to be, I never realized she was paying all that attention all that time to all that was going on around her. She's nailed the daily life of an actor in LA about as perfectly detailed as it gets.

(One thing I want to knock her sideways for is her constant use of modeling terms, like "booking" a role. Maybe its just me, but I never "booked" a role in my life and I don't think Laura has either). But other than that, she knows lots of things that without, a person could die on the Vine in L.A.; especially beautiful girls.

A word about Beautiful Girls. If you're lucky to be beautiful, and that's all, run–do not walk–out of L.A. They feed on beautiful girls out there, chew on them and spit them out. If you look in the mirror and see a beautiful girl, pay attention to to the chill wind that goes up the back of your neck, and make an oath–more than a promise, but not a compulsion–on whatever you hold sincerely in your heart; your mother's life, your sister's health, your connection to the Divine. If you're a beautiful girl, make it your business to be something more and make yourself expert and known for that. Be the best, most acute political observer. Know thyself (actors forget too easily that what makes them unique and different is ultimately their greatest gift and power) and take advantage of acting's magic. Acting is a time machine, an airship, looking at the people as God sees them.

Take a walk through your mind–that thing that is you that is as big as the Universe–and realize that each singular shape, attitude, opinion, makes you stand out. And something happens to people when they see an actor observe herself and give what she sees to her audience; they close a circuit, as Laura once said, and what is unique to Laura or Richard stands in for everybody–at one time familiar and totally eccentric; she is always her, I am always me and because of that we are you, which is what the name of the game is.

There is nobility in acting. In the layers of pretense an actor puts on there is the potential for authentic truth. You know this from letting yourself be moved by Spencer Tracy, Irene Dunne, Humphrey Bogart, Errol Flynn... or don't you know the names of the greatest film actors who came before now? You must, y'know; because when movies were younger they were closer to Magic and Mystery than they are now, even though we can deliver a certain tech magic that wasn't even dreamt of in the old days. But if you want to be an actor, don't leave out the parts that were written with wit and wisdom, and had to carry the Not so special effects that now are "yo, baby, Perfectly Special," and for no particular goal...

Laura is a brain with a body. She can act outside of her century, like I'm betting we'll see in her next film by Tarantino. She can look around and find you and smile, and suddenly you're in 1845... and at the same time be taking in the cables and cameras and interaction or lack of same between director and actor...

You can say that Laura is amazingly correct in everything she says and sees, but she makes you hunt for the urgent need to to do it which is at the bottom of all. She is a rarity in that she knew exactly what she wanted and figured out the price for it, and when it got too high and her soul was part of the negotiations, she knew what was important for herself–when so few do and give it away. And then– what do you have, when they come for the gem you're capable of showing, and you've "thrown a pearl away?"

Introduction

This is the book I wish I had found when I was seeking a guide for the amazing adventure that has been my career in acting. Unlike most actors, I didn't dream of a career in showbiz as a kid. Though I inherited my family's passion for watching movies and television, it never occurred to me as a child that those people were doing a job and making a living at it. I'm a practical person who had practical dreams. It wasn't until I was 25 years old that I realized what I was supposed to be doing with my life. I quit my job managing a special occasion dress boutique, as well as my job teaching English Composition at a community college, and abandoned preparations to begin my doctorate in English Literature/Creative Writing. Then, I moved to New York to start my journey and I never looked back. That was 23 years ago. This year, after supporting myself as an actor since 1996, I am playing Leonardo DiCaprio's sister in Quentin Tarantino's *Django Unchained*, a role Quentin wrote for me.

I came to acting almost completely ignorant. I'd done a Teens Onstage production of Godspell when I was 17 mostly because my brother loved the city theatre group for years. I suspect I got the part mainly because I had a good soprano voice and could hold a "high A" for a long time. I loved the experience, the camaraderie of building something together and that feeling of touching an audience. Then I went on to college to pursue my practical dreams. I paid for college with scholarships, a Pell Grant and several jobs including 4 years as a D.J. in a nightclub. Again, I loved connecting with the crowd. I also worked as a model and found I loved the catwalk but, though I loved the audience, I saw my years as a runway model as another way to pay the bills.

I may not have known anything about acting, but with two degrees already under my belt, I definitely knew how to study and learn. I took on acting like it was college. I read dozens of books, studied at the American Academy of Dramatic Arts, N.Y. and took classes from theatre conservatories, casting directors and agents. I started doing plays and auditioning for commercials. I even did student films and a day of background work in a Spike Lee movie. In 1992, I was totally ready to move to Los Angeles and get to work. I was educated and talented now! I was surely one moment away from being discovered. At 28, I realized I was starting too old to have Julia Roberts' career but I just knew I would find people who saw my work and felt compelled to hire me.

Though I was no small-town girl, having just come from New York (and the D.C. area before that), nothing could have prepared me for moving to Los Angeles and the career that lay before me. I'm hoping this book will give you the heads-up I didn't have and help you integrate into the working culture quickly. Each time I thought I was "ready," I'd encounter some new situation no one prepared me for. There was so much to figure out. When do I join the union? What do I wear to auditions? Can I use props? What do I do if the script says to kiss someone but it's just me and a camera? What do I do if I mess up in the middle of the audition? Should I hold my sides at the audition or do I have to be off-book? Do I fill out the whole size card? Should I try to chat up the casting director or just dive into the scene? What makes a good headshot? How do I get a good agent? How do I get work without an agent? Should I give up if I've auditioned for over 100 commercials and haven't booked one yet? (Seriously).

In Los Angeles, I continued to study acting, taking scene study classes at the Beverly Hills Playhouse for several years and joining two theatre companies. I took a job tearing tickets at a multiplex so I could see as many movies as possible with an audience. An agent's wife took a shine to me and I got a summer job at a boutique agency to get a clear understanding of their methods and expectations. Socially, I began meeting movie stars, producers, studio executives, directors and other people in a position to lead me to work. This brought up a whole host of new questions. What do I say to these people? Do I mention the play I'm doing? What's the difference between networking and using people? If someone gives me their card and I email them and they don't email me back, can I email them again later or am I bothering them?

In 1995, I got my first L.A. theatrical agent and began being seen for film and television roles. By this time, I was absolutely certain I was ready to be "discovered" and start working my butt off. I booked my first part in a big Hollywood movie, the sequel to the beloved *Terms of Endearment*. Both Shirley MacLaine and Jack Nicholson would be returning for *The Evening Star* and would be joined by fellow Academy Award winners and nominees; Juliette Lewis, Miranda Richardson and Ben Johnson. I had three scenes and a filmed montage of clips working directly with MacLaine, Richardson and Lewis. It was a dream come true and certainly a launching pad for an unknown.

While filming a scene where Juliette and I were co-stars on a TV sitcom about Catholic school girls, Shirley MacLaine entered to watch her "granddaughter" (Lewis) from the bleachers. I could hardly believe I was working with this national treasure and that she was essentially a background player in one of my big scenes opposite *Saturday Night Live*'s Mary Gross and John Bennett Perry (Father of *Friends'* Matthew Perry). Then something amazing happened. MacLaine came alive as the overbearing "Aurora" and totally stole the scene right out from under us without ever saying a line. I should have known that those gold statues don't come easy. It was a crushing blow when I saw the movie and realized that was the only scene that survived their hour of cuts from the original. I was totally floored when I saw that the scene began at the very end when we all said one line each (mine was, "Bye") and then zoomed into Shirley clapping and creating a whole story of a person in just a few seconds–and with no lines. Though I was devastated at my dashed dreams, I finally really got what was meant by "**There are no small parts, only small actors.**" You can turn any minute into a moment. You can be unforgettable with no dialogue and nothing to do but clap. I watched MacLaine do it with my own eyes. I watched the choices she made and the courage she had to fill a moment with detailed acting jewels. It was a marvel to behold. From then on, I made it my mission to make every part unforgettable, no matter how small, and steal every scene I could.

I started scene study classes with the amazing Ivana Chubbuck and took Margie Haber's cold reading course. I learned how to break down a scene and deliver a unique take on material. So many more questions got answered. How can I make the scene my own? How can I stand out from the crowd if I only have one line? What do I need to know to go from being good to being great? What can I do to win out over people with way bigger resumés than mine?

When I started working more steadily, new questions arose. How do I put together my reel? When can I add credits to my resumé? How do I know if the camera can see me? Can I ad-lib? What if I hate my character? Am I allowed to bring my phone on a set? What do I do if I blow take after take? Financially, what's the best way to actually live off of such an up and down business? Do I need a publicist? How do I get dresses for the red carpet? Who do I invite to a premiere? Should I wait until I have a movie at Sundance to go there? What do I do when no one's calling and nothing's happening? How can I stand out at a commercial cattle call? How do I stay motivated? How do I survive so much rejection and failure?

Over the years, I have been privileged enough to work on movies like *Kill Bill, Enemy of the State* and *Django Unchained.* I've been on *Friends, JAG* and HBO's *Treme* and have appeared in over 50 commercials. I'm what's known as a "working actor." I'm no household name, but if you've watched TV and movies in the last 15 years, you've probably seen my face. I also wrote and directed *Intermission,* an award winning short film starring Joanna Cassidy, Julie Brown and Danica McKellar, as well as an 8 minute scene starring Academy Award Winner Richard Dreyfuss. In 2007, I produced *Hell Ride* with Quentin Tarantino starring Dennis Hopper, David Carradine, Michael Madsen and Eric Balfour. In 2009, I moved to New Orleans and a whole new set of questions opened up. How do you get started in a secondary market? How is it different? How do you network in a smaller market?

This book answers all of these questions and many, many more. I've included details as often as possible whether it's explaining step-by-step how I got a dress from *Project Runway's* Austin Scarlett for the red carpet (with him as my escort) or whether it's listing dozens of questions to ask yourself when breaking down a scene and building a character. This is the book I wanted to find when I started out and the book I needed while building my career. It's is the nuts and bolts of everything I needed to know to go from a dress boutique manager and English Composition instructor to a working actor with a long resume´and health insurance. My years in the industry have taken me around the world, introduced me to people I grew up watching and given me the opportunity to be part of America's #1 export; entertainment. I figured out how to do it at the age most women are retiring, with no family in the industry and without having theatrical representation for most of my career. I wrote this book to explain to you how to turn minutes into moments and moments into a career.

For the purposes of this book, I've focused mostly on film, though the information applies equally well to television. As they are a huge source of income in many careers, I've included a chapter that deals exclusively with commercials. Voice-overs create another tremendous revenue stream, but I recommend you find another source for this information as I've never attempted to make money in this way.

I've also taken the liberty of referring to all decision makers on your career path as "Bigwigs." Whether I'm discussing a director, a producer, a studio executive, a casting director or all four, they are the Bigwigs.

When I refer to the newly formed SAG-AFTRA union as "SAG," it's simply because that's what it was called at the time.

There are industry terms in this book. I have attempted to define many of these terms within the body of the text. If you come across a word or phrase you don't know, I suggest you get in the very good habit of looking up things. If you have trouble finding a term's meaning, comfort yourself in knowing that generations of actors figured these things out before the internet.

There are also many references to actors and movies and the occasional TV show. Some of these references are older, but not obscure. This is a book about being unforgettable and the truest way to tell if someone or something is unforgettable is to wait awhile.

Between the internet, Amazon, Hulu, vintage video stores and many more avenues to film and TV, there's no excuse for not knowing why Marlon Brando matters or why *Gone with the Wind* is still one of the highest grossing and most beloved movies of all time. Though tastes vary, I have endeavored to include a variety of references that I hope are familiar to you. If not, I hope you will enjoy discovering them.

Know Small Parts

PREPARING

Chapter 1:

Small Parts are a Big Deal

There Are So Darn Many of Them

There are many reasons to know how to make the most of a small part. As a working actor, one reason small parts are a big deal to me is that I make a living playing them. I have health insurance and a pension and a union to take up my grievances. I never made enough money to own a house in the hills, but I rented one with money I made as an actor. I never bought a new sports car, but twice, I got a "like new" convertible that I could own outright. I'm not a household name and I'm rarely asked for my autograph but I can go to the store without makeup and reporters never go through my trash.

I'm not saying, or even implying, that you shouldn't aim for starring roles, Academy Awards and reporters in your trash. What I am saying is that you can make a living as an actor without ever achieving those goals. You can make a living doing something you love. That's a pretty big deal even for small parts.

When most actors begin their careers, the majority of roles they are in the running for tend to be on the small side. "Bit part," "under-5" and "under-10" usually refer to parts that have between one and ten lines. Most actors start out in these parts and "working actors," actors who make a living acting, often continue to do small parts throughout their career. For every star in a movie, there can be dozens of smaller parts. Think about your favorite movies. *The Matrix* had a couple of celebrities, a strong supporting cast and dozens of smaller parts. *The Dark Knight* had one Batman, a big ensemble cast and dozens and dozens of smaller parts. *The Departed, Shawshank Redemption,* and *Gone with the Wind* all have celebrities, supporting casts and very long lists of smaller parts. Maybe one day, you'll be one of the stars with your name and face on the poster, but a <u>lot</u> more people will have supporting and small parts in your movie.

Until then, as an actor's career kicks into gear, the opportunities usually expand to include bigger parts in smaller projects and small parts in bigger projects. I found that TV afforded me the opportunity to play bigger parts as a "guest star." Co-star and guest star parts can vary in size and importance. I've had parts with only two scenes that afforded an amazing opportunity to show range. I've had parts that meant something to people, like when I was Ross' first date after his breakup with Rachel on *Friends*. And I've been the focal point of entire episodes where my story was the main story all the stars revolved around.

I found that independent films could be more open to hiring an unknown in a larger part, whereas blockbuster films tended to fill their larger parts with celebrities. Think of the smaller movies that introduced us to some of our favorite stars; Reese Witherspoon in *Man in the Moon*, Scarlett Johansson in *Ghost World,* Halle Berry as a crackhead in *Jungle Fever*, Vince Vaughn in *Swingers* and Matthew McConaughey in *Dazed and Confused*, just to name a few.

Once you're a celebrity or a director, there can be "Cameos." Bruce Willis and Julia Roberts appear in the cameo-packed Robert Altman film, *The Player*, Cate Blanchett in *Hot Fuzz,* Drew Barrymore in *Scream*, Tom Cruise in *Tropic Thunder*, Alec Baldwin in *Glengarry Glen Ross* and Neil Patrick Harris in the *Harold and Kumar* movies. Throughout most careers, there will be commercials and auditions. Even when you're the star of a commercial or a product spokesperson, you're part is never longer than 60 seconds. Auditions can vary and I've had to prepare a 27 page audition, but most auditions are between 1 and 5 pages, no matter how big the part. As such, many of the same lessons that apply to small parts are invaluable to the audition process.

One reason to master small parts is that between commercials, Under-10's, cameos and auditions, there are so darn many of them. Small parts are opportunities to pack an entire person into a few onscreen minutes and create a moment.

Secondary Markets

Another reason to pay attention to smaller parts is "secondary markets," states outside of California that have up-and-running film industries. Secondary markets in the U.S. today include Louisiana, New York, Florida, Texas and more. Many states offer tax incentives for filmmaking. Find out if your state has a Film Commission and look into how much work is available.

Since most casting occurs in Los Angeles, the majority of the parts available to actors in secondary markets are smaller "local hire" parts. Someone who masters small parts and works in a secondary market can become a pretty big fish in a much smaller pond.

My first paying acting job was as a principal in a regional commercial that ran in the midwest. I booked the job through a modeling agency in Baltimore. I wasn't even a trained actor yet and I was already SAG-eligible. During my 3 years in New York, when I wasn't studying acting, I was able to get signed by my first commercial agency. That agency had a deal with an L.A. agency which gave me a contract with a commercial agent when I moved to Los Angeles. I have no idea how long it would have taken me to achieve all of that had I started in Los Angeles, but I do know that I arrived in L.A. ready to work.

After building a career during my nearly 18 years in Los Angeles, I moved to another secondary market, Louisiana. Armed with my resumé and reel, I was snatched up right away by my first choice agent. Though few commercials shoot here, and they accounted for about half of my career in L.A., I've worked steadily since arriving. On set, I meet lots of local talent. There are other working actors able to make a living here. There are also hundreds of people starting out as background and hoping to get that one line of dialogue that will turn them into a "principle actor," someone with a credit and maybe even a scene for their reel. I'm still figuring out how much work my new home affords me, but it's clear to me now that it's much easier to meet the basic requirements of an acting career in a secondary market. In a smaller market with fewer people competing for parts, it's easier to get the available work, find an interested agent and join the union. If things go well, you can even build your reel. Even if you're dying to test your wings in L.A., you might want to consider how much better you'd feel arriving there with proof that you can get hired.

They Deserve It

My favorite reason to know how to make the most of a small part is that they deserve it. No good writer ever added a character to a script for no reason. Adding a character to a script is a fairly big deal involving stopping to name and describe someone. If anyone else in the scene could have said the line, your part would never have been born. Eventually, producers will read the script. There's one type of producer, the Line Producer, whose job includes finding ways to cut money out of the script. That means that after the writer found it essential to create the part, the producers agreed it was necessary, or at least found it was cost effective. By the time you're in the audition room, everyone involved in the preproduction phase has signed onto the part being important enough to cast with someone they find "right" for the role. If all those people agree that the part is important enough to deal with step-after-step of the filmmaking process, from conception and casting through wardrobe and directing, then the part deserves your full attention.

Getting "Discovered"

Every time you work as a background player, there's a small chance you could be given a line–the line that launches your professional career, the minute that turns into a moment, the moment that starts your career. Every time you play a small part, you are being afforded an opportunity to shine. You can never know who might see it. If you do make a moment out of a small part, someone may notice you and cast you in a bigger role. My guess is that this is the most popular reason to know how to make the most of a small part, the hope that you might be "discovered." And with good reason–it's sometimes true. Almost never, but sometimes.

No Small Parts, Only Small Actors

David Carradine was in almost 150 movies and over 80 different TV shows. As such, I had a deep respect for him and am thrilled to have appeared in two of his movies. While in Cannes with *Kill Bill: Vol. 2*, we ended up in the same town car. Paparazzi swarmed the car and we were unable to move for some time. As the flashes popped like strobe lights, he told me that the movie would be very good for my career.

I laughed it off, "It'll be very good for YOUR career."

He laughed too, "Yes." Then he explained that filmmakers love Quentin Tarantino, that young filmmakers especially love Quentin and, "You never know who's watching you."

I remained skeptical, "I only have a few lines."

"Ah, but the way you deliver that, 'Mmm-huh'... That's the 'Mmm-huh' heard round the world."

These years later, I can say that most people who see movies have seen *Kill Bill*. Some of them remember "Rocket" (my character's name), due in large part to Michael Madsen's contemptuous delivery as he all but spits it at me. Some people remember the moment or the girl in underwear. But, as Carradine predicted, there are those who love Rocket and her "Mmm-huh" attitude. Some of them have been filmmakers. When the director you're auditioning for is a fan of your work–that's a good day. Yes, it was two lines and a "Mmm-huh," but those two lines continue to lead me to more work, including three more films produced or directed by Tarantino. Turns out that one of the filmmakers who was inspired by that performance was Quentin himself who ended up writing a part for me in *Django Unchained.*

But don't take my word that small parts can become big moments. Think for a moment about some of your favorite moments in TV and film, even commercials for that matter. Every opportunity to act is an opportunity to create an unforgettable moment.

Some small parts carry through an entire film, popping up to move the story forward to illuminate how another character is changing or to lend comic relief. Stephen Root's red stapler loving employee in *Office Space* only has a few lines but he pops up throughout the film lending continuity and a running joke. Jeremy Howard had a similar running gag in *Accepted* as "Freaky Student," a kid bent on learning to explode things with his mind. (Loved Howard as a Trekkie-type in *Galaxy Quest* too). But for my money, the mack-daddy of running-gag small parts has got to be Suzanne Somers as "Blonde in T-bird" in *American Graffiti.* She has NO lines, not one, but Richard Dreyfuss' character is bound to her throughout the film and we measure his journey by his reactions to seeing her. Though she never even met Dreyfuss until the premiere, the part launched her career.

Perhaps the smallest part ever is Kevin Costner in *The Big Chill.* Often, when an actor is cut from a movie, their actor friends comfort them with a reminder that Kevin was cut from *The Big Chill* yet most people who've heard of the movie are aware that he was supposed to be in it. Costner was subsequently cast in *Radio Flyers,* the fantastically fun *Fandango* and the Western of the '80s, *Silverado.* The rest, as they say, is history.

Before ever seeing Farrah Fawcett on Charlie's Angels, she'd turned a small part into a big moment in *Logan's Run.* Starting in commercials like Breck and Ultra Brite and moving into guest starring roles in TV shows like *I Dream of Jeannie* and *The Six Million Dollar Man,* she played just two bit parts in films before landing *Logan's Run*. Before the movie opened, she got a series regular part in a TV show called *Charlie's Angels*. She did a photo shoot wearing a red swimsuit and a toothy smile and sold millions and millions of posters before the show even aired. The rest is, again, history.

While on the topic of blonde bombshells, Marilyn Monroe was the queen of small parts for years. She first appeared on film as an uncredited telephone operator in *The Shocking Miss Pilgrim* (1947). She continued to be uncredited in *You Were Meant for Me* and *Green Grass of Wyoming* and played "Evie -Waitress at the Gopher Hole" in *Dangerous Years*. Things were looking pretty good when she booked a three scene part in *Scudda Hoo! Scudda Hey!*, but the part was cut down to one line before the film's release. More small parts followed until she finally caught a break with John Huston's *The Asphalt Jungle*. Though she wasn't mentioned on the poster, her picture appeared and her small part became such a hit that men lined up around the block to see the pretty blonde. The small parts kept coming, including a role as the mistress of an aging gangster in *The Asphalt Jungle,* and her sparkling turn as "Student of 'The Copacabana School of Dramatic Art,'" Miss Casswell in *All About Eve (1950)*. In 1952, Monroe played the part of "Streetwalker" in Howard Hawks' *Full House*. She was only in the film for 1 minute, but she received top billing alongside the other stars. More small parts followed until, in 1953, *Gentlemen Prefer Blondes* and *How to Marry a Millionaire* came out and the rest is... you get the idea.

The reason they say there are no small parts, only small actors is because **every small part is a big opportunity**. Only a limited, "small" actor wouldn't do everything in their power to make the most of it.

The Tools of the Trade

The tools and skills you learn for turning minutes into moments apply to all kinds of parts. If you're on a series for 8 years, you will continue to benefit from finding those moments that make your character unforgettable. It can be something as small as Ed

O'Neill's "Al Bundy" shoving his hand in his pants on *Married with Children* or as defining as Megan Mullally's high-pitched nasal voice as "Karen Walker" on *Will and Grace*. If you're a working actor, you already know that there are actors out there making better and smarter choices than you are. To help level the playing field, I've tried to include everything I learned from my successes and I've also included what I learned from my failures. The tools in this book are designed to help you whether you're attempting a "red carpet moment" or trying to survive blowing the same line 14 times. When you're a working actor, every scene you do is an opportunity to rise toward your career's highest aspirations. These tools are designed to help you find a fresh approach to material and to your career in general.

The same detailed work that can take you from a working actor to a star can take you from being a background player to a working actor. Whether you're hoping the Academy pays attention to you or that the director throws you a line, the ability to make the most of every moment you are afforded in front of the camera is a useful skill set. The details you layer into your character will inform your moments and the details you layer into your moments will define your character. The details you give your performances will define your career.

Chapter 2:

Breaking Down the Scene

Since, for actors, almost all parts start with casting, I'm going to start with the principles that apply to auditioning. Most of the tools that apply to auditioning will carry over when it comes time to actually play the part. That said, not everything you do at your audition to get a part will be useful when you do the work. The work environment is very different than the audition scenario. First of all, you already have the job and chances are, now you've had time to read the script. You may have spent some time filling in your character. You may have received professional coaching. And, you finally have real actors and props to work with, adding another layer of reality. During an audition, you have to create the environment, the era and the relationships while standing on a piece of tape with nothing in your hand but a script. I can tell you how to handle it when you have to pretend to kiss someone at an audition, but chances are that on the set you could figure it out on your own and it will be very different.

It takes time to break down a scene, time some of you might rather spend memorizing the lines or, worse, going out for a beer with friends. Find the time and make the effort to truly understand the scene and find a "unique take" on the material. You will likely never regret properly preparing to play a part, but I'm guessing all actors have suffered a long drive home after an audition (or, worse yet, a day of work), thinking of all the things they should've tried. It's true that no matter how much you prepare you may still second guess yourself the whole way home, but I promise it stings less when you know that you did your best to deliver.

I once had an audition for a lead in a studio film and I remember being intimidated when I passed a few celebrities on my way into the waiting room. The thing that calmed my nerves was that I knew I'd done what I could to go in there and get the role. During the audition, the director stopped me and smiled, "You're the most prepared actor I've seen." He was excited by my understanding of the character and my readiness to take direction. Unfortunately, the studio wouldn't approve an unknown for the lead, but the director remained impressed. He changed a small part from a male to a female and offered me a good rate to play the part. I can't guarantee that, if you thoroughly prepare for a part, it will result in work, but I do know that the director would never have fought so hard to work with me if he hadn't been so impressed with my preparation. Though I have a process for breaking down the script that is guaranteed to elevate your take on the scene and your character, if you'd like to go more in-depth, I recommend that you read Ivana Chubbuck's *The Power of the Actor*.

What is the Scene About?

When you book a part, you almost always receive a copy of the script. The script may contain plenty of information about your part or almost none, but it will give you the full story and a better understanding of its characters. When you audition, you may receive a script, but it's far more common to get "sides," the script pages being used for an audition.

When you first receive a script or sides, the natural tendency is to read your lines and start thinking how you'd "play it." Maybe you even start developing line readings, toying with how it should sound out loud. Resist the urge.

During your first few readings of a new scene, first try to digest what is actually happening. Who is in the scene? What do they want? What's at stake? When and where does the scene take place? Why does this scene exist? What is the genre? Is it a comedy, drama, satire, horror, mockumentary or some other specific tone? Sometimes dialogue will contain parentheticals that describe actions or tone, for example: (crying), (after a beat) or (tapping a pen). These directions can help in understanding the scene and how the writer pictured it when they were playing it out in their head as they wrote. That said, the writer doesn't have to play the scene–you do. Maybe your take on the material includes crying on cue and maybe not. Use parentheticals to understand what the scene is about, but feel free to find your own actions.

Sometimes there is precious little information about your character. The small parts sometimes have no personal details at all, like "Waiter." The more you understand about the scene, the richer you can make your moment, no matter how small the part or how little information you're given about your character.

Who Are You?

Hopefully, the scene contains some information about your character. Sometimes you are given a "breakdown," a description of the character and their place in the plot. But even if you have nothing but "Waiter," you have a number of questions you need to answer. You know what your occupation is, but are you good at it? Are you the best? How long have you had this job? Is this your first day? Is it your dream job? Maybe, in reality, you hate your job waiting on tables, but before you jump to conclusions about the character of Waiter, ask yourself a few things. Is this a good job in the community where my character lives? Is my character a third generation waiter at this restaurant and proud of it? Am I making good money? Am I making enough money to make me like the job even on a bad day? Is there some personal need the job fulfills for me? Do I love meeting new people or touching base with the regulars? Is the staff like a family? Is the restaurant the place I escape to because my character's home-life is awful?

The more details you explore, the more questions you ask, the more layered and textured your take on the part will become. Are you rich? Are you educated? Are you new in town? Are you married? Do you have children? Are you an expert at anything? Are you funny? Are you popular? Are you mentally stable? Can you be trusted? Are you shy? Do you have any handicaps? Are you a historical figure? When were you born? What were the customs of that time? What music do you listen to? What foods do you eat? What scent do you wear? Are you a fantasy character? What is your fantasy world like? Does your character have permission to be outlandish? Are you from another country or region? Do you have an accent? Is your character lying? Does your character know they're lying? Is your character a good liar? Even if the line is as simple as, "I'm fine," before you jump to conclusions, ask yourself if the character is really "fine" or hiding something?

When you feel you've explored the questions regarding your character, it's time to fill in the other characters in the scene and your dynamics with them. Who do you care about in the scene? How long have you known them? Are they in a position of authority over you? Are you in love with them? Do you believe them? Do you owe them money? Did you grow up with them? Are you related? Are you attracted to them?

There may be more than one person in the scene, but you usually only really care about one person's reactions to you. Are you saying things to one person hoping to impress the other person? Are you using one person to make the other jealous? Are you secretly conspiring with one person against the other? Are you competing with anyone in the scene?

It helps to understand the purpose of your character in the scene. Who are you in the scene? Are you an authority figure? Are you the punchline? Are you usually seen as a dumb hunk and this is your character's moment to shine? Is the scene happening because of your character? Do you have a clue someone needs? Do you know you have the clue? Are you the voice of reason? Are you a fish out of water? Are you a representing a stereotype? Have you always been this way or is your character daring themselves to do something new?

Think about your character's goals and aspirations. Do you get what you want in the scene? If you don't, do you get what you want in a later scene? If you get what you want, do you still want it after you get it? Did you get what you want but not the way you wanted it?

After you've questioned the scene and your character, it's time to think about your appearance and how it helps develop your character. What do you look like? Are you a sharp dresser? Are you a zombie? Do other people in the scene find you attractive? Do you accessorize? Are you stuck in the '80's? Do you wear a uniform?

The more questions you ask, the more detailed your portrayal will be. Detailed acting is what separates the pros from the rest. Detailed acting stands out in a crowd. The more thorough you are in understanding the scene, the better prepared you will be to answer questions while developing your character. You will be able to add details that create a unique take on the material. The more developed your character is, the better the odds that you can turn minutes into unforgettable moments.

What Do You Want? – Objectives & Stakes

Once you understand the scene, you can start formulating your "objective." Simply put, your objective is what you want in the scene. If you have the script, you may have a lot of information about what your overall objective is, but each scene will have its own objective. Sometimes your character states their objective out loud like, "I want to run away." Don't be fooled. Sometimes we say things we don't mean to get what we <u>really</u> want. Maybe your character really does want to run away or maybe what they really want is to make someone stop them. Maybe they're getting someone to apologize or propose. Maybe they want the other person to offer to come with them. Only by understanding the scene can you make a strong, well-supported choice.

Sometimes the ending can hold a clue. If you marry the person at the end, you want to end up with that person no matter what your words say. Your objectives will always be about ending up with them. But, don't "play the ending." Just like in life, your character may be discovering their fate and what they want as they go.

Your objective should always serve your character. Sometimes we do nice things for people, but we usually have a self-serving reason for our kind deed and that's not a bad thing. When you give someone an engagement ring, you may be selfless enough to think your objective is *I want to give her a good present*, but a stronger choice is, *I want her to marry me*. When you give a homeless person a dollar, your objective may seem to be *to help them*. You may be doing it out of the kindness of your heart, but you're not exactly changing their economic outlook. A stronger, more achievable objective than *I want to help them* is *I want to relieve my guilt* or *I want to feel better about myself* or *I want to appear generous*. Ultimately, your objective must be something you can get from the other person in the scene, whether it's love, money, respect or information. Scenes are always more dynamic when your character has a goal that involves getting something from someone else in the scene. Needing the other person makes their character important and necessary. Imagine how different a casting director feels when an actor does all they can to focus on getting their scene's needs met through them. It can create purpose and intimacy and intensity and that can be unforgettable.

Why are you here? No one talks for no reason. Your character has a reason for saying what they say the way they say it. It's your job to figure out what that is and be specific in your choices. No matter how small the part or how short the scene, every character has an objective in the scene. You may think you're off the hook if you're playing Waiter at a party and your line is, "Your martini, sir."

I would argue that having so little to build on just makes your job harder. Sure, the reason you say, "Your martini, sir," is to get the bigger actor their drink, but you are a specific waiter, a whole human being, delivering a drink. Though it is a dangerous business to make choices that might interfere with the rhythm or natural flow of the scene, it is your job to fully fill in Waiter's life and intentions.

Who are you talking to? Is the person you're serving someone you might admire? A famous artist? A war hero? A politician? Your father? Is it someone you hate? Your best friend since the second grade? Your ex? Do you know the person you're serving? Is it someone you hope will notice you?

How do you know which objective will be the best choice? Good acting is about making strong, detailed choices. There are many reasons people do what they do, but not all of them are interesting to watch. If you're playing Waiter, *I do this job to pay the rent* is a weak choice. *I do this job because I want to meet Host* is a much stronger choice. It gives you a reason, not just to be at work, but to be engaged in this particular night at work.

Once you know what you want in the scene, you need to know why? What is at stake? *I need money* is a weak choice. *I'm being evicted if I don't come up with cash* is stronger. *I'm a princess under an evil witch's spell and I need to kiss Host* is probably unsupported by the scene and is therefore weak, or worse, off-putting. A good, strong choice for Waiter is *I want to impress Host because I know he's hiring for a job I really want.* This objective gives you the critical element of wanting something from the other person in the scene as well as something at stake, something to win. The best objectives are stated in the positive. *I don't want them to leave me* is a weak, negative choice. *I will do anything to make them stay* is far stronger. Understand the scene so that you can choose strong objectives, then fill the character and scene with personally powerful details that inform that objective.

Who do You Want it From?

Once again, it's time to make strong choices. *Host is just another paycheck to me* is a weak choice. In the scene with Waiter, maybe it's clear you don't know Host. If so, choosing a Host who you want to meet or who you need something from or who you have an opinion about is stronger than choosing an anonymous paycheck.

If it's clear you do know Host, it is your job to fill in that relationship with personal details. Say the script says you're the cousin of Host. A world of possibilities open up. Maybe the two of you are rivals and the "Your martini, sir" is sarcastic. Maybe it's an engagement party and you're vying for the job of Maid of Honor at the wedding. As long as your choices are supported by the script, your imagination is your only limit. There will be details available in the scene, no matter how small your part is.

Let's say the party is in a small town and Host is someone your age, perhaps you went to school together. Maybe you had a crush on them years ago and need to know if there's still a spark. Maybe you see them as a homeowner capable of throwing parties with hired help and, feeling small in the face of it all, you need to be validated as an equal. If it's a lavish party and Host is bragging about their new yacht, maybe you hope they'll be so impressed with your professionalism that they hire you as a waiter on the ship so you can escape your life and see the world. There will be clues in the scene. Follow them to the answers about who you are, who you are talking to, what you want in the scene and what is at stake.

Substitutions

Once you know who you are and what you want in a scene, endow the other people in the scene with history from your own life. You're Waiter and your line to Host is, "Your martini, sir." Let's say Host is a congressman and he just grabbed you and kissed you moments before. First, understand the scene. If you're both men or he's married, does this mean you now know a secret about him? Your objective could be to let Host know you'll keep the secret or that you'll expose him and take him down. Think how differently you'd approach, "Your martini, sir" if it's a threat versus if it's a pledge of loyalty or interest.

Armed with an understanding of the scene and strong choices about your objective, you can examine the dynamics to assign a substitution to each character. A substitution is someone from your own life who helps fill in your history with each character in the scene. Maybe you've personally never even voted for a congressman, but many of us have been hit on by someone we were impressed by or someone in a position to fire us. Maybe you've been in a position to expose someone's big secret before. Dig through your own experiences to inform your character's experiences. Come up with more than one substitution and try them out in the context of the scene. Choose the one that lines up with your objective and creates the most interesting dynamics between the characters.

If you're playing Waiter and the strongest objective is *to impress Host and get a great job offer*, the best substitution might be the most obvious. In real life, you want to impress the Bigwigs and get the gig. The casting director might make an excellent substitution. Even if things go badly, you can use that to work even harder to get what you want. I try to remember this no matter what my substitution is. An inattentive casting director can be a great motivator. Substitutions fill in emotional history but, ultimately, you have to react to the actual person in front of you.

Details and Research

The more details you layer into your work, the better your chances of creating a unique take on the material, maybe even an unforgettable take. Details from your own history, relationships, preferences, passions, goals and physical appearance can fill in a character and their history, relationships, preferences, passions, goals and physical appearance. These are the details that bring your character to life, give them history and help you create a take on the material that's unique to you.

Once you've explored the details of who you are and who you're talking to, it's time to add more layers. The objects, places and other people in the scene need to be personalized as well as those mentioned in the dialogue. Let's say that Waiter has two lines, "Your martini, sir" and "Your wife would like to speak to you." "Wife" is not just some generic congressman's wife, she's a whole person with an entire history that includes speaking to you and telling you she'd like to see her husband. If the congressman just kissed you in the hall, maybe you're lying to put him in check, but assuming you're telling the truth, you interacted with Wife and have some opinion of her. Finding a substitution for Wife from your own history will fill that interaction with personal details.

Any object or place in the scene or the dialogue is another opportunity to personalize the scene. Maybe you've never been to a gala in a ballroom, but you've probably attended someone's fancy wedding or at least a prom. Maybe your character's never been in a ballroom either. Did they always dream of being in a room like this? What fancy room have your always wanted to be in? There may not be a whole lot of room for personalizing a martini (unless, of course, it's poisoned), but there may be other objects in the scene. Maybe the script says, "Waiter checks their pocket watch." Who gave you the watch? Was it the congressman? His wife? Your grandmother? What does it mean to you? Is is a good luck charm?

Maybe this seems like more detail than the scene calls for and loading up a scene with details can be distracting, but in real life, you do it all the time effortlessly. You wake up in a place that means something to you on a bed you may have shared and pass objects and photos full of memories and history. You drive a car that may have been your first car or a graduation gift or a symbol of your hard work or status. You talk about people who aren't in the room and bring them to life because they are worth mentioning. And you do all of this without acting it out. All of those details and all that history are simply part of your world, your scenes in life.

Details can be found in occupations. You might also benefit from researching certain occupations like an undertaker or a magician. If the part calls for an occupation like waiter, you may already know that the job may include doing things like cutting limes or rolling silverware in napkins. Understanding what people do all day at work gives you material and plenty of details for actions and improvisations. When I was preparing for the role of "Masseuse" in *For Love of the Game*, I got a professional massage from someone I knew and asked lots of questions while observing her technique. I noticed she would wipe a dollop of cream onto her forearm. As she massaged, rather than having to reach for more cream as she worked, she'd take some from her arm and keep going. I used that detail and have been thanked by quite a few masseuses who appreciated the realism. A couple even thought I must've been a pro. That detail created a reality of that masseuse's world and the way she does things–as smoothly as possible.

Maybe you can't work a day as a spy, but you may be able to reach out to one who wrote a book about it. Maybe you can't assist in a surgery, but you might have a doctor or at least know someone who's had surgery. The great thing about movies is that most people love them and pretty much everyone watches TV. Generally speaking, people like talking about themselves. Imagine how delighted your accountant uncle might be to help you get a gig by talking about himself. A lot of information can be found online, but the most authentic details will be found in real people being themselves. Try to experience your character's occupation somehow, then ask lots of questions and pay attention to behaviors. People can be a treasure trove of details.

Sometimes you can <u>create</u> a detail and add it to a scene or character. While preparing for *Django Unchained*, I realized I wanted Lara Lee to have something equal to the men's guns, a feminine "weapon" of some kind. Django and his cohort, Dr. Schultz, were both quickdraw artists. I thought it might be cool if Lara Lee was a feminine quickdraw artist. I came up with the idea of Lara Lee's fan. Lara Lee would be armed too, but armed with a lacy fan she could snap lickety-split. I trained for a week before initially presenting the prop to Quentin for approval to move forward. Then I trained for 2 months before presenting it on set in costume with the prop fans that had been designed and prepped. The entire time, all those hours of planning, prepping and practicing, I didn't know if the fan would even make the cut, but I did know one thing–if Quentin liked it, I was ready to deliver. Once Quentin approved the fan trick, I layered fans into all of Lara Lee's scenes. It became my defining detail for her character. Though we shot the scene differently, in the original script, Lara Lee was supposed to take a gun from Dollar Bill knowing she had no idea how to use it to defend herself. By the time she would have to relinquish the fan for the masculine gun, her feminine weapon would have come to mean something to Lara Lee and, I had hoped, to the audience.

*Note: As of this writing, I have still not seen *Django Unchained* but I have heard the fan trick didn't survive the last grueling week of cuts and that is, of course, disappointing. Two lessons I've learned come in handy at times like these. One is to remember that the fan detail helped anchor my reality as the character so, though none of my fan moments may appear, the work I did on that idea informed lots of the other choices I made that will make it to the screen. Second, every time you think you've done enough work or found enough unforgettable moments, it's important to keep working at layering more details and choices into your work. Save nothing–use everything. Your can't control which moments will make it through the editing process but you can give the Bigwigs lots of strong choices. Delivering one moment they can't live without will help your odds of survival and may even help save your entire storyline.

Django Unchained is a "period piece," a project set in another era. When you approach a period piece, in addition to understanding the scene and filling in the objectives, substitutions and details, you may also need to do some research. If you're playing a real person, living or dead, you will most certainly need to investigate the facts of that person. Thank goodness for the internet. When I was starting out, we had to go to the library with a fistful of dimes to print the copies.

When playing another era or country, it might be important to know all sorts of things. Be curious. What do you eat? Are you literate? Can you vote? How many children would you normally have? What wars and disasters did you watch unfold? Do you have electricity? How long can you expect to live? Investigate everything from inventions of the time to popular songs and books. You may not be asked to participate in the wardrobe/hair/makeup decisions, but it may still be important to familiarize yourself with the "look" of that era. When I realized I'd be wearing a hoop skirt in *Django Unchained*, I borrowed one from wardrobe so I could practice walking around in one without knocking things over. I figured out how to sit and curtsy. I found my stride and posture and got comfortable with the hoops weeks before I wore one on set. I filled my iShuffle with songs from Lara Lee's lifetime. Lara Lee is a widow so I researched occupations her husband might have had and how we spent our time during courtship and marriage. Finding the details helped me make strong choices to build the character and history of my dead husband, our life together and what led to his death. I would have done all the work even if it was only for myself, but when it came time to shoot, I ended up being able to use it for dialogue when the script called for Lara Lee to improv "holding court" at the dinner table.

If you know who the actors you'll be working with are, you can make an effort to establish relationships with a few of them. Before filming *Django Unchained*, I was able to meet several times with Dana Michelle Gourrier who played my slave and confidant "Cora," as well as Dennis Christopher who played "Leonide Moguy," our family's lawyer who we grew up with. Dana and I even dared to walk around the neighborhood in our practice skirts. We prepared for walking on rough terrain, navigating narrow throughways, walking side by side or holding hands, all things mentioned or implied in the script. We even practiced walking with her holding a parasol over me, just in case it came up. Did we feel silly? Of course we did. I was wearing a Saints football fan shirt and a white nylon hoop skirt. I felt like an idiot. I can't imagine what the passing tour busses thought of Dana holding a floral umbrella over me on a sunny day, but we both felt ready for work when the time came. When we found out that our first day of shooting would be walking up a giant staircase with our skirts in one hand and flaming candelabras in the other, I think we were both glad we'd gotten comfortable in our practice skirts.

If you're playing a real person, many of the details of the person may be available to you. Birthplace, significant dates like graduations, weddings and children's births, even photos or images may all appear online. But the meat of a person can only be guessed at by reading "facts." Cleopatra, Martin Luther King, Jr. and George W. Bush have all been well documented, but in order to play them, you'll have to dig deeper than the story of them. As with characters from other eras or countries, you might find it helpful not only to find their behaviors and mannerisms, but to create a scrapbook of their lives or a record of their thoughts. I like to create an autobiography complete with photos. Once I've written about my birthplace and circumstances, I try to answer every question I can think of. I write about my character's family, friends, pets and co-workers and how I feel about all of them. I write about my goals and dreams, my favorite memories and what I care about. With those details in place, I start a journal of my character's thoughts and reactions in the scenes. Since we mostly shot *Django Unchained* in order, a rare and wonderful treat, I continued journaling as we shot. As cast changes and new ideas altered the scenes, I incorporated them or wrote about my reactions to the changes.

Do all the research, but remember that it's a movie. If the director tells you to do something "historically inaccurate," let go of your research and find a way to create a moment without it. It's true that you might do all this work just to end up on the cutting room floor, but any muscle you exercise gets stronger. Exercise the muscle of being ready for anything. Then, when your moment to shine arrives, you'll be ready.

Moment Before and Obstacles

Another layer to explore is obstacles. What is standing in your way? Staying with the role of Waiter and the objective of *I need to impress Host and get a great job offer*, what might prevent you from meeting them in the first place? Perhaps your scene would benefit from creating a "moment before." The moment before you walked up to Host, what were you thinking? How have you come to be in the scene? What led you here? What happened right before this scene? What mood are you bringing into the scene? Were you optimistic? Were you nervous? Were you confident? What were you doing? Were you praying? Were you reciting affirmations in your head? Were you rehearsing what you were going to say? (Be careful with that one, it's best for comedy). Were you humming? Were you stealing a taste of the martini? (Again, careful, this involves resetting props and all kinds of continuity nightmares for many people so it better be worth it). Were you waiting for the right moment? Were you making sure the martini was perfect?

What obstacles did you have to overcome to arrive there? Was it raining? Were you supposed to be somewhere else? What choices did you make that led to this scene? Does your character want to be there? Do you know what's going to happen next before you walk in?

So, Waiter crosses the room and offers Host his martini, "Your martini, sir." This is an opportunity for obstacles. I say opportunity because obstacles heighten conflict and conflict is the stuff of storytelling. You may only be offering a drink, but you are part of a story and, as we've already established, you are essential to its telling or you wouldn't be there. Within the story the film is telling and the story the scene is telling is the story of your character. Maybe only you will ever know all that went into Waiter, but backstory can create details, substitutions can create details, a moment before and obstacles can create details, and details can create unforgettable moments.

Maybe Host is talking to other people when you walk up and you have to wait so as not to offend him. Now you have the conflict of feeling like an obedient dog in front of someone you hoped to impress. Or maybe you can barely contain your excitement and the longer you have to wait, the harder it is to contain yourself and appear normal. Maybe you're waiting while he's talking to someone privately and you have to avoid appearing like an eavesdropper.

Maybe Waiter's part is strictly limited to walking up and delivering a drink and a line. There's still room for details. If you understand what's happening in the scene, create a backstory and substitutions and a moment before, then when you deliver the drink, you'll know whether Waiter smiles at Host or avoids eye contact or winks or nods knowingly. You'll know whether Waiter bows his head when he offers the martini or hands it over begrudgingly to an obviously drunk man. Use all the information given in the script and fill in the rest with your imagination, observations, research, practice and personal experience.

Conflict often comes from competition. When you set your objective, you are setting the standard for "winning" the scene. In the case of Waiter, we set the objective of *I need to impress Host and get a great job offer* and the substitution of *I need to impress this casting director to launch my career*. Using the casting director as your substitution may be a good shortcut and even give you a way to use your nerves in the scene, but focus on the realities of the scene using the substitution to fill in specifics and details. Sometimes we don't fulfill our objective in a scene, but we can still "win" the scene. *Detroit Rock City* is an entire movie about four guys getting to a concert so most of the movie they do not get what they want, but you have to believe after every defeat that the guys will eventually make it there. Every obstacle they face, every defeat they suffer, the guys continue to persevere. The effect is sort of intoxicating. Watching the film, I noticed that I started to really care whether the four slacker dudes made it to the Kiss concert or not. Silly, right? But, the actors sold me with the lengths to which they were willing to go to win. It's how you get what you want that makes people interesting. Once you know who you are and what's at stake, you can develop a unique take on creating and overcoming obstacles.

Obstacles can be created from a moment before or something in the script or an inner conflict or a dynamic between characters. If you fail, even overcoming failure can create an obstacle. One of the many, many great moments in *Gone with the Wind* is when Rhett reveals himself to have been eavesdropping on Scarlett throwing herself at Ashley–and being turned down. She tries acting like a lady who is shocked by his behavior. When he laughs at her, she attacks verbally. He comes right back at her, so she plays the victim and accuses him of taking advantage of her. He's not falling for it, so she insults him. He mocks her so she storms off. She may have lost the scene but she won his heart and ours by being resourceful, tenacious and funny.

Moment After

In the room you will not know whether or not you got the job, whether the casting director is going to launch your career. In the Waiter scene, you walk away without ever saying anything more than, "Your martini, sir." Not exactly career launching conversation. Now it's time for a Moment After. Like the Moment Before, there's no guarantee anyone will ever see all the work you've done on your Moment After, but you have to keep acting until the director yells cut or you leave the scene. No exceptions. Think about your reactions to the exchange with Host. Are you disappointed? (Be careful–this can be a weak choice). Are you giddy? Do you feel proud of yourself? Are you embarrassed? Do you hide your face as you walk away? Do you overcompensate by waving goodbye or bowing repeatedly as you go? Do you spin your tray like a pizza? Do you make the sign of the cross? Do you sigh? Do you untie your apron? If the scene is limited to delivering the drink and leaving, do you spot someone off-camera who needs a drink? Do you remember something you had to do in the kitchen? Every detail helps to create a moment and if the director catches you doing it, they may decide to use it.

Pulling It All Together

I've heard people say they thought they'd be good at acting because they were able to memorize things quickly. A quick memory is always an asset, but if that's all it took, I know a few Academy Award winners who would be out of a job. Marlon Brando supposedly had lines taped inside his coffee cup in *The Godfather*. Acting is hard work. Great acting can be grueling. Memorizing lines might be the easiest thing you're called upon to do and no one pays money to watch someone recite a memorized script.

Take the time to break down the scene. Figure out what the scene is about and who you are. Choose a strong objective for each scene and figure out who you want the objective from. Fill in substitutions and details and do any research necessary to play the part. Fill in your moment before and obstacles to heighten conflict and develop a moment after to complete the scene.

Do you have an original take on the material, the dialogue or the character? Does it all make sense? Are your choices the strongest ones? Have you tested them? Remember that it's <u>how</u> you get what you want that makes people interesting. Maggie Smith can change your worldview with an arched eyebrow. Have you found your moments to shine? Make strong choices, test them out and be ready to adjust and nail the scene "as written" and you should be ready to turn any minute into a moment.

Chapter 3:

Taking It To the Next Level

Once you've pulled it all together, it's time to take it to the next level–delivering. By now, you should have an original take on the material filled with personalized details. Having a complete understanding of the scene, you've developed an objective that drives the scene forward using both the text of the scene (what it says) and the subtext (what's really happening).

All the preparation in the world isn't going to amount to much if you don't deliver when the camera starts rolling. The best way for Bigwigs to figure out if you can kill it on camera is if you can bring it at the auditions. Though much of this chapter applies to delivering on the job, I've focused on auditions as they are the key to getting the job.

Focus

Acting requires a tremendous amount of focus. You have to be able to block out anything that might interfere with your performance while remaining open and alert to anything happening in the moment. In a Bigwig's office, this may include ignoring phones and chatter and a wandering dog WHILE being open to reactions to anything the reader is giving you, trying to bring up tears and reacting to being stabbed. On set, focus will definitely include ignoring lights and equipment and hundreds of people while trying to deliver an unforgettable moment.

Every actor has techniques for focusing. Many do relaxation exercises or listen to a particular song or look at an object that evokes emotions. Some run their lines over and over like a meditation. Some actors can find their focus quickly while others need to stay in character even when they are not on camera. Find something that works for you. When the cameras roll, anything can happen. Learn when to ignore peripheral noises and distractions and when to let things that happen affect your choices in the moment. If a piece of equipment crashes off-camera or a plane flies overhead ruining the sound, ignore it until someone yells, "Cut." If an object falls on camera, it would be unnatural to ignore it and you will have to instantly figure out what your character would do in that situation at that moment. While filming the dinner scene in *Django Unchained*, Leonardo DiCaprio slammed his hands down on the dining table take after take until, during his explosive speech, he accidentally slammed his hand down onto a tiny cocktail glass on the table. The glass cut him deeply enough to require stitches. He decided his character would continue making his point, allowing the dripping blood to increase the passion and darkness of the moment. Or maybe he's just a consummate pro who never stops acting until he hears the word, "Cut." Either way, it took the scene to a whole new level and was truly unforgettable.

Judging

Sometimes you luck out and your character has a lot in common with you. Sometimes their circumstances are similar to your own. But, often, you are playing someone you seem to have very little in common with. Either way, the most genuine performances come from truly connecting with the character, their circumstances and their motivations. What if you don't "like" your character? Sometimes you're asked to play people who are criminals or idiots or liars or adulterers, even murderers and rapists. When I started out, I thought I'd be playing love interests and young lawyers, teachers and camp counselors. Instead, I've played two strippers, a zombie, two adulterers, a slave owner, a serial killer and two hit-men. I also played plenty of love interests and some young professionals, but many of my characters turned out to be "bad guys."

I actually find it a lot more fun to play someone I have very little in common with–someone I would never be who does things I would never do. Not only can it be fun, I find it soul enriching to walk a mile in shoes I find so unfamiliar. Everything good parenting and therapy would tell you not to do can be helpful in finding the motivations for bad behavior. The key to combatting judgement is justification. Hitler had his reasons. They may have been sick and twisted, but they drove his choices and helped him sleep at night. Justification comes from righteousness and blame. You HAVE to do the things you do, because of what was done to you and/or because "they deserve it."

Instead of fighting your idea of the character, ask how it is that you would end up just like they did. In *Kill Bill, Vol. 2*, I played Rocket, the head stripper at a middle-of-the-desert strip club. Though I had ideas about strippers, I suspected many of my impressions were stereotypes. Rather than fighting the idea that I would be a stripper, I asked myself how I would've ended up in a nowhere town supporting myself in this way? What would put me in this strip joint in this job with these people? Not some actor version of me, the actual real Laura. What choices would I have had to make to get me here? Rather than choosing negatives, it's always best to look for active, positive, winning choices. I looked at the moments when I made wise choices and asked what would've happened if I hadn't? What if I had dropped out of high school or gotten into drug abuse or some other downward-spiral set of choices? I asked myself who I was loyal to in the scene? Who in my life would I have followed to the ends of the Earth? Whose happiness would I have made more important than my own? Immediately, I knew there had to be a man involved. I came up with a fairly elaborate story of how I'd come to not only live this life, but choose it. By empowering my choice to be a stripper in a nowhere club, I was able to not only imagine myself in this scenario, but to own my power as a stripper. Instead of "ending up" a stripper, I chose active objectives that strengthened my character and justified her behavior. As Rocket, I chose to be a stripper out of loyalty to someone who'd been influencing my choices for years. Being a stripper became an empowering choice. The result was a truly head-butting scene between Rocket and Michael Madsen's "Bud." Quentin later told me, "I've always kinda prided myself on my ability to pick the right actor for the right part. And, uh, you're the Joe-mother-fucking-Louis-of-the-under-five-in-her-underwear and I was able to get Joe-mother-fucking-Louis-of-the-under-five-in-her-underwear for that part."

In class, I often heard actors say, "My character would never do that." Never? Never ever? I wondered how they could know their characters so well in only a week? I've known myself my whole life and I can still be surprised by what I "would do." And I've lived long enough to know that I was born into middle-class circumstances and all the benefits that provides. As life got tougher, I became more resourceful. If I'd been born with less advantages or different surroundings, I might have used that resourcefulness to be a better criminal or a more clever seductress rather than a good student or a loyal daughter. The bottom line is that your character WOULD do whatever it is because that's the way it's written and it's your job to figure out why.

The less you judge, the more you can illuminate the truth of a character. Don't need to be liked, need to be unforgettable. Instead of asking how you can become like this person or act like this person, ask yourself how you <u>are</u> like this person. Character actors are able to disappear into a role leaving only the slightest trace of their own ego. Some examples would be Gary Oldman in *The Contender*, Sean Penn in *Dead Man Walking* or *Milk or I Am Sam*, Jamie Foxx in *Ray*, Whoopi Goldberg in *The Color Purple* or even Emma Stone in *The House Bunny*. That said, most parts you audition for will call for your type, even if only in a general sense.

It would be easy to judge someone who kills people. But our job is to bring our characters to life. Rather than focusing on how you would never kill anyone, focus instead on why your character would, why you might if you were in different circumstances. Don't judge–justify. Justifying your character's actions and ideals doesn't mean you have to subscribe to them, it just means you have to make it real for yourself. My serial killer on *Diagnosis Murder* was killing people who'd been brought back to life. She believed that when they died and came back, they brought something evil with them because she'd had a personal experience of that circumstance. Rather than pondering the question of killing being wrong, I set my mind to finding a similar belief in my own life.

It's important to remember that your justifications must be things that help you to "win" the scene. When I was in Ivana Chubbuck's class, I went through a phase where she kept assigning me victim roles. After six or seven of these in a row, I went to Ivana and asked her to give me a scene where I wasn't a victim. She gave me a scene from *A Streetcar Named Desire*. But rather than playing the tragically charismatic "Blanche DuBois," I was to play "Stella," the spouse-abuse victim. I asked Ivana how long I'd have to keep playing victims. She said, "Until you quit playing them as victims. " Ahhh.

I used my make-up skills to make bruises, including finger marks on my arm from where I imagined "Stanley" grabbed me too hard and left his mark on me. Rather than judging or getting stuck on what I would or wouldn't do, I played the scene as a woman in love with a man, a woman who knew she had a magical hold on that man and a woman willing to get hit to make sure she had his full attention. It felt totally different, way more fun, and I never had to play another victim. I'm still asked to play victim parts, but now I see them as people so determined to meet their needs that they lose sight of their welfare. That's something I can relate to.

Have Fun, Show Off

Remember when you were amazing in your living room? The point of an audition is not to get the job, it's to show the Bigwigs what you would do if you did get it. I'm going to say it again. **The**

point of an audition is not to get the job. Only one person is going to get the job, but everyone being seen is being given an opportunity to make a lasting impression. Many of the small parts I've done have come from auditioning for lead parts I didn't get. Twice, after not getting a part, people who were already filming decided to write a part for me to include me in the project.

You're not in control of whether or not you get the job. You can't know what the Bigwigs are looking for and many times, they're not really sure until they see it. I have a theory on this called "the philosophy of purple shirts." When I was starting out, I spent a lot time trying to figure out what the Bigwigs might want. I'd read the breakdown, if I could. I'd read the parts of the sides that were crossed out, hoping to find my character mentioned. And I'd pay special attention to descriptions like, "20's, a blonde beauty but a real smart cookie."

Let the torture begin. Do they mean early 20's or late 20's? Is she a Grace Kelly blonde beauty or a Pamela Anderson blonde beauty? When they say she's "smart," do they mean she's educated or street smart? Does "smart <u>cookie</u>" mean she's Hillary Clinton smart, or that she's smart for a blonde beauty? Though these questions need answers, you can't know what the Bigwigs want. The answers to these questions and more can be found in breaking down the script, not in mind reading and second guessing.

The philosophy of purple shirts is that there will be times when people are buying red shirts and times when people are buying blue shirts, but you can't please them all by selling purple shirts. When you're breaking down the scene and developing the character, you can't know whether the Bigwigs are buying red shirts or blue shirts that day, but they are never, not ever, buying purple shirts. In other words, you may play it "big" on a day where the Bigwigs were looking for subtle or a Pamela Anderson smart cookie on a day where they were looking for a Hillary Clinton smart cookie (or vice versa), but they were never looking for someone trying to please everyone, someone afraid of failing. Your job is to come up with a solid and original take on the material and show it to the Bigwigs. That's all you truly control. I once walked into a callback where I was the only person with white skin. I had been white at the first audition so I knew it wasn't a mistake. I could only surmise that the Bigwigs were looking for someone else but they were open to my take. They didn't hire me, but the casting director started to bring me in more after that. I consider that a successful audition even though I wasn't hired.

It's not your job to know what the Bigwigs are looking for or understand why they'd bring you in for a part you're not really right for. It's your job to be a professional, instill trust in them and show them what you would do if given the part. As a professional, you have to show up on time, prepared and ready for anything. Maintaining a positive attitude and being able to handle what's thrown at you shows the Bigwigs that they can trust you to deliver on the day. Once you've done the work and the research and the rehearsing, then it's time to have fun and show off.

It is possible to have "fun" playing someone who's dying of cancer. The fun doesn't come from the material, it comes from feeling ready and open. The fun comes from letting go of nerves and watching yourself and worrying about whether the Bigwigs like you or not, and just being in the moment and connecting with someone.

There's nothing unique or interesting about you really wanting the job. All actors want all the jobs. Even the jobs actors don't really want to do, they at least want to turn down. And everyone has the same material you do, the same information. It's up to you to decide whether you're a Grace Kelly blonde beauty or a Pamela Anderson blonde beauty based on your goals, substitutions and actions in the scene.

When I was auditioning for *For Love of the Game,* I read for three different parts; a waitress, a hotel manager and "Debbie," the tan, blonde Florida masseuse. I figured I had the best shot at the hotel manager or the waitress, but they were both smaller parts than Debbie. I wore a button-down shirt for the first 2 auditions then unbuttoned my shirt exposing a tank top for Debbie. It wasn't going to turn me into Pamela Anderson, but I had made some very strong choices about her relationship to Costner's "Billy Chapel" and their history together. Instead of trying to play the part based on a few words that implied she was a beach bunny, I dug deeper into the scene and found a longtime on-again-off-again relationship under her lines. When I got the part, the Bigwigs dropped the Debbie name and Kevin added a line about liking her. Voila, Debbie, the Pamela Anderson-alike became the friends-with-benefits but ultimately disappointed "Masseuse."

Rather than focusing on what the Bigwigs are looking for or whether you are "right" for the part, invest your energy on digging deeper into the scene and finding your original take on the material. Once you know what you are saying, who you are saying it to and what you want from them, you can relax into the scene and enjoy showing the Bigwigs what you came up with. When I auditioned for *The Way of the Gun*, I went all out. From my wardrobe choice of workout gear with pounds of bling, to opening my audition singing a nursery rhyme that wasn't in the script, I knew I was either going to book the job or the director was going to laugh his butt off wondering what the heck I was thinking. I don't usually feel the need to go for broke in this way, but I had a very clear idea fully supported by the script so I took a chance. I didn't get the part, but the casting director absolutely loved it and admired my bravery. Compliments don't pay the rent, but I had a great time having fun and showing off my ideas. I left there feeling very good about myself and loving my job. To this day, I still consider it one of the 10 best auditions of my career.

An audition is an opportunity to show the Bigwigs what you would do if you got the part. If you go out on a limb, always be ready to do it as written or try another take entirely, but dare to go out on a limb once in awhile. I've left many auditions wishing I'd done something more but I've rarely left an audition wishing I'd done less. Dare to fail. You already don't have the job so it's not like the Bigwigs can take it away from you.

Watch Others

As I said before, I learned a lot from watching Shirley MacLaine on the set, but I've also learned a lot watching Ms.

MacLaine acting in such amazing films as *The Trouble with Harry, Irma la Douce, Steel Magnolias* and *Postcards From the Edge*. *Postcards* is actually filled with great small parts too, like Richard Dreyfuss as the doctor who pumps Meryl Streep's stomach or Oliver Platt as an overzealous producer or the part that launched Annette Bening, the loose and chatty background actress "Evelyn Ames." She had us at "Endolphins." When a movie is this good with a cast this strong, I try to watch it a number of times and study the performances. I feel it's very important to study the masters like MacLaine, but I feel it's just as important to focus on the scene stealers and the novices. Conrad Bain is wonderful as the grandpa who "heard that." Gene Hackman delivers a layered and history-laden performance in just a couple of scenes. Movies are the cheapest, most fun acting class you can take. TV too!

If you want to be a painter, normally, you learn the general rules and study the masters before trying to express your own vision. Same goes for musicians and mechanics, carpenters and cooks. Acting is a craft and must be learned and practiced. Think of movies and television as classes at a university. Study performances. I once saw *Gypsy* on Broadway starring Tyne Daly, then snuck in during intermission months later to compare it with Linda Lavin's portrayal of the same character. I did the same thing with the Broadway production of *A Few Good Men* as they went through several cast changes.

If movies and TV are college, then you can choose your classes. Want to learn about actors who became stars in their first or second roles? Watch Madeline Kahn in *What's Up, Doc?*, Edward Norton in *Primal Fear*, Dustin Hoffman in *The Graduate*, Lauren Bacall in *To Have and Have Not*, Sean Penn in *Fast Times at Ridgemont High*, Brendan Fraser in *Encino Man*, Lou Diamond Phillips in *La Bamba*, Sissy Spacek in *Badlands*, Ice Cube in *Boyz n the Hood* and Marlon Brando in *A Streetcar Named Desire*.

Want to learn about turning a small part into a big career? Watch Brad Pitt in *Thelma and Louise* and *True Romance*, both Samuel L. Jackson and Halle Berry as crackheads in *Jungle Fever*, Geena Davis in *Tootsie*, Emma Stone in *Superbad*, Zooey Deschanel in *Almost Famous,* Khandi Alexander in *CB4* and Jack Black in *Bob Roberts.*

Some classes in college are survey courses covering a wide variety of specifics under one topic. There are some films filled with career-launching parts. *Dazed and Confused* featured Ben Affleck, Matthew McConaughey, Milla Jovovich, Cole Hauser, Parker Posey, Jason London and Renée Zellweger among others. The cast of *American Graffiti* includes Richard Dreyfuss, Ron Howard, Cindy Williams, Harrison Ford, Kathy Quinlan, Mackenzie Phillips, Suzanne Somers and more. Selma Blair, Eric Balfour, Jenna Elfman, Jerry O'Connell, Breckin Meyer, Melissa Joan Hart, Clea Duvall, Jason Segel, Jaime Pressly, Donald Faison, Freddy Rodriguez, Sean Patrick Thomas, Seth Green, Peter Facinelli, Ethan Embry and Jennifer Love Hewitt are among the cast of *Can't Hardly Wait.* The 1982 release of *Fast Times at Ridgemont High,* featured newcomers Sean Penn, Jennifer Jason Leigh, Judge Reinhold, Forest Whitaker, Eric Stoltz, Anthony Edwards and Nicholas Coppola, who later changed his name to Nicolas Cage.

Some classes are advanced learning taught by experts in the field. It doesn't matter whether you gravitate to the movies of Meryl Streep, Morgan Freeman, Jack Nicholson or Judi Dench, you can most certainly learn from their expertise as actors. Maybe Maggie Smith's movies aren't your cup of tea, like a class you're not all that interested in. Get over whether or not you love the movie and try watching *First Wives Club* to see her steal scenes with a tiny part, or *The Prime of Miss Jean Brodie* to see how she got that Oscar, or *Gosford Park* to see how she got her sixth Oscar nomination or *Downton Abbey* to watch her rule the roost with the tap of her cane.

There are even specialty classes. Want to learn how to act with an inanimate object? Watch Tom Hanks turn a volleyball into a best friend in *Castaway.* Want to learn how to turn a dog into a costar? Watch Will Smith in *I Am Legend.* Want to learn how to skate the razor-thin line between brilliance and buffoonery? Watch Warren Beatty in *Bulworth.* There are very few new stories so chances are, if your role calls for it, someone else has already done it. Certainly you don't want to imitate anyone, but watching others can spark your imagination. If you loved the details in the performance, what details might define your character? If you were impressed by the gutsiness of the performance, what could you dare to try with your character? Even when you watch a bad performance, you can learn from someone's mistakes. Why isn't it good? What would you do differently?

Keep enjoying TV and movies, but try to pay attention to why you like what you like. You can learn a lot about what makes a great performance by watching the greats at work.

Make it So They Can't Sleep

When I was starting out, Richard Dreyfuss gave me some impossible-sounding advice. He said to, "Make it so they can't sleep. Make them stay up at night thinking of how to put you in their movie." Honestly, I thought he was probably out of touch, that the industry was more corporate now, less intimate and much harder to break into. I pondered what he'd said but it sounded as elusive as Zen, like the more you tried, the further you'd get from your goal.

My next audition was for the part of "Ellen" in *The Evening Star*. It was a small part so I was reading the sides for the character that would later be played by Juliette Lewis. I gave veteran casting director Jennifer Shull goosebumps and got the callback where I met writer/director Robert Harling. He had me do the scene over and over. He asked me to do it "angry," then "sad," then a laundry list of other adjectives. It was like he was enjoying seeing what I might do next, like he was playing with me, working with me. I left there certain that I'd booked the part, that no one could do more with Ellen than I had. When I got the call about a month later, I couldn't wait to hear the news. Then, impossibly, my agent said I didn't get the job. Luckily, about 5 minutes later, my commercial agents called to say I'd just booked a week in Paris for a commercial and billboards working with five César-winning director, Bertrand Blier. I licked my wounds and packed for my trip.

I enjoyed Paris immensely but it bothered me that I had been so certain I was Ellen. When I returned from France, my agent called and said, "You know that movie you didn't get? The director can't sleep at night so he wrote you a part."

I never doubted Richard's words of wisdom again. It became my new goal–make it so the Bigwigs can't sleep at night thinking of how to put you in their movie. When I didn't get the lead in *Krippendorf's Tribe,* the director changed a male part to a female and overpaid me to say yes. After auditioning for a lead in *Meeting Daddy* and not getting it, the producer and director shot the whole movie without me before realizing they needed me for the new happy ending. I even had a part written for me by someone who I'd met once when he joined my friend and me for coffee 7 years earlier.

Like most actors, I have lots of stories of the great parts I almost had, the game changers I almost booked, the big fish that got away. I don't have much to show for those parts that came so close. But, the auditions that left the Bigwigs wanting more, those auditions for leads that turned into offers for smaller parts, those have built the spine of my career. It takes humility to accept a few lines after having dreamed of a lead across from a star, but humility does not mean being humiliated, it means being humble. That's not a bad thing.

If you want to be a movie star, you're going to have to be more than just an actor, your going to have to be unforgettable. Ultimately, an actor is someone who plays parts but a movie star is someone who makes total strangers fall in love with them. Some people call it the "it factor." Dan Hedaya is an amazing actor who stars in lots of movies but Tom Hanks is a movie star. It doesn't matter if an actor is more talented than Anna Faris or Jackie Chan (both of whom are hugely talented), we love our stars. If you're a natural-born star, if you've always been unforgettable, then know that you are enough. Maybe one day you'll learn to play the lead in *Erin Brockovich*, but Julia Roberts won our hearts in the bathtub scene of *Pretty Woman* with little more than a personality as bubbly as the tub. If you are Johnny Depp or Natalie Portman or Will Smith, you are enough.

If you don't have the "it factor," then build on your type, own your power as that type, and just be the very best actor you can be. Aiden Quinn, James Spader, Rebecca De Mornay and Embeth

Davidtz all have classic good looks and plenty of talent but never really caught fire as movie stars. William H. Macy, David Keith, John C. Reilly and Kathy Bates have all starred in movies but are primarily character actors. Many character actors, because their parts are smaller, are able to do far more projects of a much wider variety than their movie star counterparts. The good news is that you don't have to be able to make us love you just by getting caught singing in a bathtub. If you can make it so the Bigwigs can't sleep figuring out how to put you in their movie, you can build an entire career out of smaller, high-impact parts.

A lot of actors think that they are totally ready to be leads in movies and that they are "one part away" from becoming the stars they were meant to be. Maybe so, but I thought this for years and now I see things differently. Some people do get "discovered" very early in their careers. Most do not. For most working actors, it takes a long time to build a career. Looking back, knowing what it takes to do this job, I don't think I was as ready as I thought I was–maybe even by a fairly long shot. It wasn't until I was on the set of *Flipper* that I realized I didn't know how to walk a tracking shot with a multitude of marks. It wasn't until I was on the set of *Friends* that I realized I knew nothing about working in a three-camera environment. At that point, I was really only ready to fake my way through and learn as much as I could while trying to deliver an unforgettable performance. I was ready to work with Oscar-caliber actors, but I wasn't ready to truly stand my ground, much less steal the scene from them. I wish I had spent less time convinced that I just needed a break and more time focused on making the most of the breaks I got.

~⚬ WORKING ⚬~

Chapter 4:

Audition Tips

When people ask me how to become an actor, I ask them if they like job interviews. Until you're at the level of stardom that warrants offers, you're going to have to audition for most of the parts you get. If you are very, very lucky, for every job you book, you will go on at least 10 auditions, sometimes many, many more. If things go well at the audition, chances are you'll be rewarded by having to do it all over again in front of more Bigwigs at the callback. I've had to audition 3 times for the same part on several occasions, including once for a commercial. But, I booked it.

The problem the Bigwigs are hoping you will solve is the answer to their question, "Who's the best choice for this part?" Not the best actor, the best choice. When I wouldn't get a part, sometimes my manager would say I "wasn't their strongest choice." I didn't really understand what that meant until I started casting my own project, *Intermission,* a short film starring Joanna Cassidy, Julie Brown and Danica McKellar. I precast those roles without auditions knowing that the actors would bring their considerable talent and fresh ideas to their roles. Then we set about casting the other parts. Some of the strongest actors we saw weren't the right energy for the part, some weren't the the right age range. I was trying to create a very diverse ethnic palette and that came into play when filling in some of the smaller parts. Some actors were eliminated simply because I had too many of their type already in the scene. But, I can say with all honesty that I sincerely hoped each person that auditioned would be "the one," the one that would solve my problem of "Who's the best choice for this part?"

You may not like job interviews. That will be your cross to bear. It doesn't matter why the Bigwigs called you in, it's an opportunity to leave an impression, to be memorable. If you can find a way to enjoy auditions, you will have a much more fulfilling experience of your career. We actors don't usually have a "job," we have careers. Yours is happening right now. Whether you're a seasoned pro looking for tips in this book or just starting out and not even in the union yet, your career is happening right now. You are already an actor and, if you've been paid, you're a professional actor. Those of us who make a living at this are working actors and precious few of us become stars. Auditions are our opportunities so the more we have, the better our career is going. Until you become a star who gets offers, you will almost always <u>have</u> to audition WAY more than you <u>get</u> to work, so it's a good idea to find a way to like it. I try to remember that I don't HAVE to audition, I GET to audition. When I'm sitting in traffic, changing clothes in my car and fighting over parking spots, I try to remember how many actors are sitting at home wishing they had my problems. I try to remember how many more are sitting on couches watching TV, saying, "I could do that." Auditions are opportunities. Be an opportunist.

Before my nearly 18 years in Los Angeles, I was in New York for a few years. I got a high-powered commercial agent through my modeling agency. I was attending the American Academy of Dramatic Arts, learning everything I could about the craft of acting, and attending dozens and dozens of Broadway plays to learn by watching. I read book after book and watched movies like I was studying them for college. But I didn't know much about being on film and I knew even less about auditioning.

My agents were great at sending me out. They were patient with my learning curve, convinced I would eventually make us all some cash. As time wore on and I got better at the process, they started sending me out for more and more dialogue-driven parts. I suited up, showed up and did my very best every time. I was tireless and my agents kept giving me more opportunities.

The first 30 auditions were fairly discouraging. I only got a few callbacks and didn't book even one. To make matters worse, my beyond-gorgeous roommate who'd never acted a day in her life went in for her first audition, a national network commercial starring Paulina Porizkova. The Bigwigs were looking for someone who looked just like Paulina and booked my roommate the next day. It was pretty discouraging. That said, she never booked another spot. We all have our own race to run.

The next 20 auditions were more of the same disappointment, but I trudged on. Once I crossed the "50 yard line," I began to feel discouraged. I started noticing that I NEVER booked these things, not once. Sure, I'd done one regional commercial in D.C. before I ever started my career, but not one commercial since becoming an actor.

The next 20 auditions were harder. I started getting discouraged when someone would walk into the waiting room and I recognized them as someone who worked a lot, or worse, a celebrity. I called them the "Oh Fuck" girls, the people who could make a whole room of actors say to themselves, "Oh fuck" just by walking in. They were ringers, working actors, pros and my competition. I started wondering if I'd EVER book a commercial. Worse, I wondered if my agents would lose faith and drop me.

But an interesting thing happened when I crossed the 90th mark. I started wondering what I would think of my 90th audition if I'd already booked my 100th. If I knew in advance that I would book my 100th audition, wouldn't I be thrilled to be getting the 90th one out of the way? Wouldn't it just mean I was one step closer to my goal? I call this, "The Lesson of the 100 Auditions."

The truth is that if you want to be an actor and be happy at the same time, you've got to learn to live with rejection. Ideally, you want to learn to love rejection, to want to eat it for breakfast and ask for more. If you truly believe that you are doing what you were called to do, if no other job fulfills you as much as acting, then rejection is just the path to the work. If you focus on having a great audition rather than on booking the job, you can do everything in your power to turn the opportunity into something fruitful and feel successful. Focus on being unforgettable and you may succeed even when you fail to book the part. You can't control whether you are "the strongest choice" or the solution to their problem, but you can make the most of your moment and at least get put into their file for future parts.

After over 100 auditions, I never did book a commercial in New York. When I moved, I signed with my agent's L.A. agency partners and started auditioning again. At first, I went out a lot, but after a few months, I noticed that I was only auditioning for one casting director. I took a chance and asked him if he might know why I wasn't auditioning for anyone else. He explained that he always requested me. He said my agency actually already had a version of me and their loyalty was to her. I asked him which other agencies he liked. He listed five. Then I took one more chance and asked if he'd mind me using his name in the cover letter, saying that he'd spoken highly of their agency. I knew from my summer working reception at an agency that having a reference on your cover letter was one of the things that could get your mail past the reception desk (another is making sure you address the mail to one particular person). The casting director said that it would be fine to use his name so I went home and drafted five letters. The one advantage to not booking anything for over 90 days is that you can leave your contract with your agency. Almost overnight, I had three appointments. I met all three agencies and fell in love with Kazarian/Spencer/Ruskin &Associates (then Joseph, Heldfond & Rix). After over 100 unanswered New York auditions, I started booking almost immediately and stayed with KSR the entire time I was in L.A. Over time, I became an "Oh Fuck" girl and, even as I aged in and out of categories, the commercials just kept on coming.

It would have been easy to get frustrated after 100 "failed" auditions. I could've even justified giving up. If I'd known all those auditions were just preparation for a lucrative and lasting career, it would've been a lot easier to see them as opportunities to learn and get better. The truth is acting requires a lot of faith, believing something is possible when you have no proof. Any muscle you exercise gets stronger. Exercise the muscle of breaking down scenes, of being a pro and of daring yourself to make bold choices. You can't know which jobs you'll book, but you can look at every audition as an opportunity to turn minutes into unforgettable moments.

Be a Pro

Never be late. If you're running late, call your agent or manager and let them know as soon as you see the writing on the wall. When you arrive, remember that <u>you</u> are responsible, not traffic or alarms not going off. Apologies may be necessary, but excuses are never welcome and, trust me, hardly ever original.

You're trying to instill confidence that you are the right person for the job and that the Bigwigs can count on you to deliver on the day. As such, it's not okay if your phone goes off during your audition. If you can't be professional when it's all about you, how can they count on you when you're just one of the many moving parts on a set?

It's better to have a headshot and not need it than to need one and not have it. It's also not a bad idea to have your reel available somewhere online in case someone wants to see it.

I remember standing in a parking lot once when a Santa Ana wind rolled through. I noticed the street lamps swaying. I realized that in order to be truly strong, strong enough to withstand earthquakes, the lamp posts had to be flexible. Things are often out of your hands in this business, especially in an audition situation. Be yourself, be strong, but remain flexible. Be open to direction without seeing it as criticism. Be willing to embarrass yourself. Remain upbeat and willing. Roll with punches and try not to take things personally. Remain focused on your objective in the scene no matter what happens in the room. Remember that the Bigwigs called you in. It doesn't matter why they called you in, it's an opportunity to leave an impression, to be memorable. Use each opportunity wisely.

Know Which One You Are

There are two important aspects to knowing which one you are. First, you are the one who wants the job, the Bigwigs are the ones who can get you that job. Therefore, your phone is dead to you. They can take a call or text but you shouldn't even use a vibration mode. Why would you build a possible distraction into the audition? Unless you are waiting to hear if your wife is going into labor, turn off the phone. The Bigwigs can keep you waiting. You cannot keep them waiting. In some restaurants in L.A., you can tell who wants something and who has what they want just by who arrives at the table first. Choose your battles. Being kept waiting is not usually a battle worth getting into (though it is okay to engage your representation to do a little fussing if things get out of hand).

The second aspect of knowing which one you are is knowing how you are perceived by the industry, which "type" you are. It's an ugly, but necessary, truth that many jobs are cast by a type: tall 40ish doctor-type, buxom 20's blonde-type, geeky teen-type, Jewish mom-type, jock-type, rapper-type, etc. Again, choose your battles. It doesn't matter to the Bigwigs if it offends you that you are typecast as mature (meaning old) or overweight or slutty or even dumb as a bag of rocks. It's not their problem if you don't like the box they've dropped you into. As I see it, you have two choices–attempt to change the box or cash in on your quirks.

I haven't gotten to audition for entire categories of jobs simply because I was tall or too young or too old. The smart move is to drive into the skid. Those of you who drive in snow or standing water know that, when your car spins out of control, you don't yank the wheel in the other direction, you drive into the skid and regain control. I am tall but tall is good for lots of parts. If I know I don't have to read next to anyone, I feel perfectly comfortable wearing heels. Tall women evoke several kinds of parts–models, fantasy figures like angels, and women we instinctively "look up to" like politicians, doctors and judges. Tall women can also be gawky, nerdy, outcasts and oddballs. The one thing tall women can't be is shorter than Al Pacino. If the part calls for a shorter type of woman, don't take it personally. Put it in your rearview and keep on truckin'. You have to believe that for every part you are too bald or too urban for, there will be a part you are uniquely perfect for simply because you are not the norm. Learn to embrace your freckles or big bones. Tina Fey has a scar across her cheek. Kate Bosworth has two different-colored eyes. Harrison Ford's nose is crooked. Even the beautiful are imperfect. There is room in this industry for Melissa McCarthy, Verne Troyer and John Salley. Roseanne Barr and John Goodman made a hit show out of lacking glamour and class. Know your type and own it.

There will be times when you can change Bigwigs' minds about what type the character should be. The original types for *Lethal Weapon* were a white suburban dad and a black suicidal drunk. But most of the time, you were called in because of your type. Sure, your resumé matters but the Bigwigs are not even going to turn the photo over if you don't look right for the part.

Some actors worry about being "typecast," playing the same part over and over. Honestly, unless you have a successful career with options, you should probably worry more about getting cast. Throughout your lifetime, your type will continue to evolve. Jodie Foster was a freckle-faced kid until she did *Taxi Driver*, when she became more edgy. She played grittier and grittier parts until she spiked the ball with *The Accused*. Having taken gritty as far as she could, she then began playing smart people befuddled by life and that type has continued to evolve into tough broads; some wielding weapons, some wearing stilettos and wielding power. I have no doubt that as she enters her 50's, she will continue to cover new ground as an actor and as a type.

Kurt Russell spent the first 10 years of his career under contract to Walt Disney as a spunky kid but, with *Escape from New York*, he became a badass. He then became a romantic lead able to bring the funny. By the time he was cast in *Tombstone*, he'd already proven his ability to be the right guy for nearly any type of leading man role and he's been dancing around the genres ever since. But, most of us will have to know what we're selling and if Kurt Russell hadn't been typecast as a spunky kid for a decade, we may never have heard of him. Maybe now Neil Patrick Harris can play everything from a womanizer in *How I Met Your Mother* to himself as a out-of-control celebrity in the *Harold and Kumar* movies, but his typecasting as a smart kid in *Doogie Howser, M.D.* led him to sincere and resourceful roles like *Snowbound: The Jim and Jennifer Stolpa Story*. His performance as the husband trying to outwit the elements showed that he could be trusted with heartfelt smart-guy roles. I've even seen him play a psycho or two but he was always a type. Now he's the adult edgy, funny version, but he is still essentially the smart kid now grown up.

Some people find an acting groove and mostly stick to it. Clint Eastwood may be a young cowboy or an old man who lives next door, but he's always the "make my day" guy. Eastwood is a tough guy. Woody Allen is the neurotic guy. Jack Nicholson is the cool guy. We count on them to deliver those goods. Sigourney Weaver delivers as a tough broad. Goldie Hawn is still adorable. Never mind that she was smart enough to produce many of her movies starting with *Private Benjamin* and the fact that she's now deep into her 60's, her kookiness still delights. Like politicians, these people remember to please their base.

The point is that even the actors who are typecast can have enviable careers. The trick is to know what you're selling, drive into the skid and stick around long enough to become relevant again. John Travolta went from being the cool kid in *Welcome Back, Kotter* to a sex symbol in *Saturday Night Fever* and *Grease*. He'd been an *Urban Cowboy* and a goofy new dad in *Look Who's Talking* before he remade himself as the adult version of the cool kid in *Pulp Fiction*. In the nearly 20 years since then, he's played a governor, an officer, a bunch of bad guys, even a woman (*Hairspray*) while growing into his new type as a middle-aged cool guy. He will probably continue to evolve on film, able to play parts like those Paul Newman chose later in his career as well as comedies like those Jack Lemmon chose.

Jessica Lange started as the beautiful sexy blonde clutched in King Kong's grasp. Without ever losing her grip on the sexy blonde-type, she evolved into the soap-star-next-door in *Tootsie*. She moved on to tragic beauty parts like *Frances* and grieved with dignity in *Men Don't Leave*. By her Oscar win for *Blue Sky*, she proved she could even make lunacy sexy, feminine and magical. In her 60's, she's playing a creepy fading beauty in *American Horror Story*.

Sometimes the ego plays tricks with the brain. When my commercial agents moved my age range into the 30's, my ego whispered, "I can still pass for twenties, I just got carded last month." At first, I had trouble competing in the category. A lot of the other women had been competing in the 30's category for awhile and some looked more like mom-types than I did, which is a big chunk of the 30's category. My ego whispered, "See, I look too young for this category." But my ego doesn't run my business so I reminded myself that I was already 31 when I did my first film playing the 20 year old "Sitcom Actress Becky" who was playing a 17 year old on a TV show. I'd been in my 30's for a long time before anyone brought it up. I trusted my agents that I would grow into this new category. Soon, I was booking commercials again and a whole new world of parts opened up to me.

It may be no fun to hang up your belly-baring tops and micro-minis or your logo'ed t-shirts and Ed Hardy, but if you've aged out of a category, you are only hurting your best opportunities by letting your ego tell you how to dress. Helen Mirren still looks great in swimwear but she probably takes meetings in slacks. Keanu Reeves can still pull off a tank top, but he probably wears sleeves to meetings. Yes, youth is critically important in the industry but, like it or not, you are going to age. The question is whether you will continue to evolve as a type as you leave child actor-type or young hottie-type. You may lose work by aging, but if you drive into the skid, you may find, like Joan Allen, Johnny Depp or Robert Downey, Jr., that your best career years are as a "grown-up."

Have the courage to be what you are and know there is some kind of work for every type of person. Perhaps *Precious'* Gabourey Sidibe isn't a classic leading lady, but tell that to her Oscar nomination in a leading role. Hollywood has been home to giants and little people, the deaf and the wheelchair-bound. If Marlee Matlin can be a leading lady and Verne Troyer can have a career, you can find work even with mismatched ears (like Stephen Colbert) or hit your peak at 90 (like Betty White).

Get over yourself. Figure out what you're selling and keep it simple. I used to want to show the Bigwigs my range. I wanted them to see how I could shift from my complicated self into this very different character. The truth is that it can be better to leave the Bigwigs with one simple, memorable impression than a laundry list of things that make you great. You only have a few minutes so pack them with power, not personality changes.

And though the Bigwigs are often stereotyping you, you would be wise not to stereotype them. The first time I sat on the other side of the audition table was as the writer/director of *Intermission*. Also in the room was my producer, Nicholas M. Muccini, and a female reader. All of the parts were for women. We met over 50 women and I noticed a funny thing, the vast majority of them only looked at Nick until they found out I was directing. Many continued to defer to Nick even after they knew. Perhaps this will change over time, but for now, we tend to assume that the men in the room have the power. I realized that perhaps I did this too without knowing it. Ever since then, I try to remember that the youngest person in the room could be the director, the woman could be the producer. I know a segment producer who looks like a male fantasy with long ringlets of hair and well-displayed breasts, but she knows what she's doing and is respected for it. Brett Ratner was 28 when *Money Talks* came out, so he had to be even younger when he held those auditions. You never know who you're talking to. Like everything else, leave your prejudices and preconceptions at the door. Be aware of how the Bigwigs see you and be very careful how you see them.

Chatting

Often, when you enter a room, there's some small talk encouraged. I'm pretty good at small talk but it can be treacherous terrain. I once complimented a casting director on a photo of her and her mother. Only it wasn't a photo of her with her mother. The younger woman I thought was the casting director was actually her younger sister and, the older woman I thought was her mother was actually the casting director–which means I complimented the casting director for looking like a woman old enough to be her own mother. Oops. There was nothing to say, no way to fix it. She never called me in again. Unless someone looks like they have a basketball shoved up their shirt, don't assume someone is pregnant and ask when they're due. And though some people are hoping you'll notice their snow globe collection or the photo of their child, remember that every person who's ever walked into that room has seen the same objects so try to be personal with your observations. "You like snow globes?" is a closed question allowing only a yes or no answer. Try "Is this your only collection?" or "How long have you been collecting these?" or "Is one of these the first one you got?"

You may want to share that you love the director's work or some other compliment, but this is not about you being a fan, this is about making the Bigwigs a fan of yours. Telling someone how great they are isn't a very good conversation starter as it generally limits their response to, "Thank you."

Unless I've already met the Bigwigs before, I usually try to limit opening chit chat. If I'm nervous about the audition for any reason, I may offer that we just dive right in if they don't mind. I also try to keep closing chatter to a minimum, especially if I feel I did well. You certainly don't want to end a strong audition with a comment about their dog's photo only to find he died 2 days ago.

When you've been in the industry awhile, you'll get to know some of the people you're auditioning for. In this case, it's fine to catch up a little. A side effect is that nothing rattles a waiting room full of competitors like sitting through an audition that takes a long time and includes laughter or hugs. That said, you've been the one waiting and checking the clock. Have mercy on your fellow actors and leave the Bigwigs wanting more.

Questions

It's fairly standard for the Bigwigs to ask if you have any questions before you audition. The time for most questions to be answered is before you arrive at the audition, but if you wondered how a name was pronounced or some other simple question about the text, this is the time to ask. You are expected to know how to pronounce any words you could just look up. You are expected to know the meaning of every word in the sides.

If you're not sure who you'll be reading with, it's best to ask. If there's a chair there and you'd prefer to stand, ask if they'd mind. Don't, however, assume that they will follow your actions with the camera. If the camera is set up for standing and you'd like to move around, ask if they'd mind. If you want to use a potentially frightening prop, like a weapon, ask. Definitely ask.

If you don't have any questions, find some way to pass on the moment without sounding like you haven't worked on the material. Humor can be helpful. Try something like, "I had it all figured out in my living room, so I'm optimistic," or something to that effect.

Listening

At some auditions, you will be given instructions. Listen closely to what the Bigwigs want from you. If you're given a list of tasks or marks, try to remember them all and in the right order. Play it all out in your head. Rehearse mentally. Especially at commercial auditions, you may be directed to look at a Post-it note stuck on a light and think a thought, then pick something up and interact with it, then cross to a mark, then put the thing down, then deliver your line. Listen to all the directions. Play them all out mentally, then do your best to deliver.

Sometimes the Bigwigs will give you an adjustment. Listen closely. If you're not sure you understand, try to clarify things. Ask them to repeat it or explain, or you can repeat it and ask if they think you followed their ideas. Usually, when the Bigwigs give you an adjustment, they want to see more of the same but with the note added. If you saw the character as a diva and they say to play it less "bitchy," they're not asking you to play her like a church mouse, they just want you to make her more likable. They want you to add likeability to your diva.

Listening is also a very important part of any scene. Remember, your character doesn't know what's going to happen next, what anyone will say next. At an audition, when it's not your turn to talk, the camera is still on you. These moments are opportunities for you to fill the character in, to flesh the character out. Really listen to each line the other person says. If you doubt how much acting you can pack into listening, watch Keanu Reeves' performance in *The Lake House*. There's a scene with Reeves sitting on a porch with Sandra Bullock. He listens to her talk for over 3 straight minutes. The camera never moves and the shot never cuts. It ought to be the most boring cinematic moment in the history of film. Instead, we watch Keanu finally meeting the woman he loves for the first time. We see him relating to her, being delighted by her, making decisions about her through specific gestures and expressions. It's beautiful and unforgettable.

There are many things that set the "truly great" apart from the "very good," but being a good listener is certainly on the list. Smaller parts often have moments of listening. These moments are opportunities to set yourself apart from the very good and do something unforgettable in its detail. Let the lines affect you. Listen and let the other person's lines compel you to say your next line or do your next task or have a reaction.

In *Boogie Nights*, there's a poolside argument between Mark Wahlberg and Burt Reynolds. Center screen, in the background between the arguing men, stands Philip Seymour Hoffman taking it all in and reacting. Like a child watching parents fight, he flinches and winces all while sadness overtakes him. It's powerful, human and unforgettable–and he never speaks a word.

Being a good listener is so important that it's worth practicing. I noticed that, sometimes in real life, when someone else was talking, I'd find myself focusing on what I wanted to say next. I realized that this is not good listening. Listening means focusing on the other person, on what they say and what they mean. I decided that thinking about what I'd say next was a habit worth breaking. I practiced by repeating what people would say to me in my head. I try to ignore the noise of "Oh, I went there, I have to tell them about it," or, "I won that award too–twice," or, "This will be funny, I gotta remember to make this joke." I white-noise all of that racket in my busy brain by simply focusing on what someone is telling me and repeating it in my head. Sure, it means that sometimes, I don't remember to tell the joke or tell them that I went there too, but it's well worth it. People appreciate feeling heard way more than they care about whether you vacationed where they did once. There's also the added benefit of it making you more likable.

My acting coach, Ivana Chubbuck, once told a story about a party she went to. She tried an experiment of not talking about herself all night, just actively listening to what people had to say. The next day, the host of the party called and asked what she'd done to make everyone like her so much. Apparently, the host had received a number of calls about her charming and unforgettable guest, Ivana. I tried it myself and got similar results. I still talk a lot, probably more than I need to, but I am a much better listener now that I focus on what people are saying more than what I'm going to say next. As an actor, it keeps me from thinking about how to deliver lines and focuses me on being in the moment.

Sides

As a general rule, if you're auditioning, you are not expected to be off-book. Holding the sides serves as an indicator that is a work in progress and you are still open to direction. That said, always know your first line and last line by heart. Starting with strong eye contact and words that come naturally instills trust and raises interest in the rest of your audition so that, hopefully, the Bigwigs won't fast forward through you on the tape. Finishing strong leaves a good taste in their mouth and may leave them wanting more.

Just as in real life, try to maintain eye contact as often as possible and check in to see that you are being heard, that your words and actions are landing. You may need to read from your sides at times, but try to lower your eyes, not your head. Sometimes the auditioner will keep their eyes buried in their script or looking into the monitor. Just as in real life, sometimes if you're having trouble getting someone to look at you, you have to step it up. Invest deeper or try a new tactic.

Sometimes you're given sides for someone else's part. If Waiter has the martini line and another line in another scene, the Bigwigs may feel it's better to have you audition with one of the lead's scenes rather than a line here and a line there. Is it a bummer to do the extra work of preparing a longer scene knowing that you aren't being considered for that part? Maybe, but anything is possible. During the pre-production phase of *Kill Bill*, there was a table reading of the script. Ricardo Montalban had been cast in the part of the Mexican pimp, "Esteban Vihaio," in what is now *Vol. 2*, but he was unable to attend the read-through. Quentin asked Michael Parks, who was playing "Sheriff Earl McGraw," to fill in. If you've seen the film, you already know that Parks ended up in the role and that his work in that one scene was nothing short of brilliant. After turning in yet another dazzling turn as Earl McGraw (Parks played the same character in *From Dusk Till Dawn* and later in both *Planet Terror* and *Death Proof*), Michael Parks metamorphosed into the unrecognizable Esteban and left his indelible mark with small details including the suave and creepy way he seemed to never blink or move his lips while speaking. Another reason to get excited about doing the extra work is because you are being given a much better opportunity to shine by playing a better developed part. Let go of what you can't have and look at what's being handed to you.

Sometimes the Bigwigs give you someone else's sides because your part (and the script) is still being written. This may mean they don't have a clear idea of what they're looking for, but that could work in your favor if you're Danny DeVito or a tall redhead. In this case, you're being given an opportunity to draw the character for the Bigwigs, to allow them to see you in the part without competing ideas. Perhaps they will end up writing the part with you in mind making you much harder to beat for the role.

Sometimes, particularly in high-profile movies, the script is secret and can't be used for the audition. I recently read three scenes from *Misery*, taking on the Academy Award winning Kathy Bates' role. I was tempted to focus on the ridiculousness of the task, but everyone else got the same sides I did. Focus on breaking down and personalizing the scenes and showing the Bigwigs what you could do if you played the part. If you can find a detail that also might work for the part of Waiter, all the better.

Sometimes you're given sides for more than one part. On the plus side, this may be an indication that the Bigwigs really want to work with you. That said, it's a lot of opportunity coming at you at once. The good news is that you get more times at bat. If you were nervous for your first take, you're guaranteed another chance to shine. This is actually the only circumstance I can think of that almost guarantees you another take at an audition. You also get an opportunity to show some range. Be careful here. Don't impose contrasts for the sake of showing range. Make strong choices based on the characters and the characters will end up being different enough to notice.

On the potential downside, it's very tough to be unforgettable as one character so it's twice as demanding to be unforgettable in two and it may be an indication that the Bigwigs have no idea what they want. Take the time to break down each set of sides as if they were the only part you were auditioning for, but prioritize. Which part is the one you know you could do the most with? Which part do you have the best chance of booking? Which one do you want the most? Work hardest on the part you value most and think you have the best shot at getting. Anything can happen and they may be running late or have already cast one of the parts before you arrive. If the Bigwigs only have time to see one of the parts, forget about all the "wasted" work and focus on hitting a home run with the one part. Leave your disappointments at the door and be ready for anything.

Actions

You will be asked to do many strange things at auditions. I've had to fake showering a few times, once in milk. For my *Diagnosis Murder* callback, I had to mimic strangling someone to death. At a JCPenney commercial callback, I, along with five other people standing on a line, was asked to pretend to speak German (all of us at once) then pretend I was a chicken and jump up and down. I'm pretty sure the director was just enjoying his position of power, but I got the gig and ended up doing four commercials for JCPenney over time.

It's easy to get caught up in judging the audition as stupid or poorly managed or whatever, but each audition is an opportunity to do what you love for money. Find a way to tell the story then fully commit. If they ask you to sip an empty paper cup and pretend it's hot coffee, commit to the "sip and cum" shot. (You sip, take a short beat, then let joy and comfort wash over your face). Remember, no one is ever buying purple shirts so fully commit to every action.

This does NOT include touching things on someone's desk or throwing objects or pulling out prop guns or lighting cigarettes. Though there are stories of people doing insane things at an audition and getting the job, for the most part, scaring people doesn't instill trust. Trust is almost always good.

Sometimes a script will prompt you to kiss someone. I find the idea of miming this action too silly so I've developed a cheat. I kiss my hand or my finger and offer it to the person in some way. Sometimes it works to blow the kiss, sometimes it's better to mime putting the kissed finger to their imaginary mouth. Whatever you decide, commit fully and keep eye contact with the auditioner. Kissing is about touching but it's also about an exchange between people. Be specific and you can create the intimate exchange with your eyes.

It can be hard to figure out where to look when there is more than one person in the scene but only one reader delivers all the lines. I try to place all the people in the scene. Using the reader as the primary costar, I place the rest of the people logically. If one of them is supposed to be sitting next to me and another person is next to the reader, that's where I turn my gaze no matter where the dialogue is coming from. It may feel weird sometimes but try it at home on camera and you'll see that it plays well.

If the script says to leave at the end of the scene, leave the scene, but not the room. The scene ends when the Bigwigs say it does but you can fill every second of it as you go. Just like your moment before, you must decide what happens after the scene as well and play out your moment after.

Think out several possible actions ahead of time in case the room isn't as you'd envisioned it or you're not allowed to get up from your chair. Limit hand movements as they can be distracting and may bounce on and offscreen. Keep your sides out of the shot as much as possible. They are large and white so they will stand out if your gesture with them a lot, or worse, hold them blocking yourself. You want to be unforgettable. Don't compete for attention with your sides or any prop. Choose a few key actions and focus on getting them to land.

Permission

There's an old saying that it is better to ask forgiveness than permission. Though it is risky to live this way, there is something to be said for making bold, original choices and sinking or swimming with them. Sean Young infamously dressed as Catwoman and pushed her way onto a lot to try to get the part in the next Batman movie. Her career all but died after that. But the history of Hollywood is littered with stories of people who took a chance and were victorious. It is rare that we regret "going for it." It is common to wish we had dared. L.A. traffic is chock full of cars filled with people wishing they'd tried this or that at the audition they just left. Better to risk being Sean Young than to be a purple shirt no one wants or remembers. A friend of mine once said, "Save nothing, use everything." Don't wait to be great. Open with the good stuff and build from there.

Though it is wise to adhere to the general rules of not touching the Bigwigs or their things during a scene and not pulling out a gun or stripping your clothes off, there are times when you just have to damn the torpedoes and risk having to apologize. If you find you've gone too far, do apologize for creating discomfort. Again, humor can be useful, but an apology should never be glib. Try something like, "I'm so sorry I upset you. It made way more sense in my living room." If you've gone too far and upset someone, take responsibility for your choices, no excuses.

Sometimes you may feel the need to stand up to a casting director. Maybe the director told you he loved the way you laughed and at the next callback, the casting director tells you not to laugh. I don't suggest butting heads with a casting director. Try it their way as if it was the only take you were going to get. Once that's done and done well, you can tell the casting director that the director had mentioned a few notes and ask if you can do it once the way the two of you discussed. Give to get. If the casting director doesn't want to give you the extra take, remember that it might be better to have them be the reason you don't get this one part than to make an enemy of a casting director and lose out on all their future projects.

Sometimes you can feel that the audition isn't going well. It is usually a bad idea to stop and ask to start over, but if you are going to stop, there are a few general rules. If the audition is going well but things in the room are not (phone calls, forgetting your lines, etc.), generally you want to keep going. If the audition itself sucks, only stop if you are absolutely certain you can do it <u>way</u> better right away. If you stop, there's always a chance the Bigwigs will stop the audition right there, thank you for your time and send you away with no more chances. If you are absolutely certain you have the scene ready to go and just got off to a bad start, then it might be worth risking. Think of shows like *American Idol*, where we see people doing a mediocre job then asking to sing another song. They say things like, "I know I could do it if you'd just give me a chance." Here's the thing, they had their chance. Asking for another chance after you just blew your first one is not a great strategy. That said, if you're pretty sure you're tanking the audition and you know you'll torture yourself in the car the whole way home, then it might be worth it to risk stopping the audition and asking to start again. If the Bigwigs have already worked with you or you have a reputation for being "good," you will probably find that they have compassion for bad takes. If not, you're rolling the dice.

Callbacks

Auditions require preparing for the part, suiting up, showing up (which usually includes traffic and parking) and delivering. Getting a callback means having to do all of that all over again, but that's the good news. A callback means the Bigwigs liked something they saw. Maybe it was your take on the part or your "essence" or your obvious skill as an actor or maybe they just liked your look. Whatever it was, the Bigwigs saw something that made them want to see more–more of the same. It also means your odds of being chosen have increased. You are competing with far fewer people. Maybe it's down to just you and one other person, maybe it's between you and fifty other people, but it's far fewer than they started with. They like you. They're hoping you'll solve a problem for them. They are on your side (usually).

As a writer/director or as a producer, I've been on the other side of the table a few times auditioning people for parts. Sometimes someone looks so very right for the part that you find yourself praying they can act at all, even just a little, enough to work with. As the actor, you may botch the audition and still get a second chance just because you are so much what the Bigwigs had in mind for the look. They want you to get it right so much that they're willing to let you suck a little bit and learn on film. This is especially true for commercials and one of the reasons that commercials are a good way to break into the business and its union.

There are other times when you look nothing like the Bigwigs imagined but you delight them so much with your take on the material and your general demeanor that they open their minds to a new possibility–that the character may look exactly like you. But most times you are getting a callback because you have the right look for the type, you were on the right track with your take and they'd like to see it again. Sometimes the director wants a chance to work with you, to get an idea of how well you take direction. Sometimes they want to watch you interact with another actor at the callback. In all cases, the Bigwigs want to see more, more of the same.

For callbacks, you should have more facility with the script. The words should come more easily, giving room to enrich performance choices. Getting a callback means you are the right type or the Bigwigs liked you in the room or you did a good job. You can't know why you've been called back but know that they are rooting for you for some reason or you wouldn't be there. I once made the mistake of asking why I'd booked a Mazda commercial. At the callback, I'd had to play out a scenario then jump on a trampoline. I was sure my background in gymnastics had helped me book the job until I found I wouldn't be one of the people jumping for joy. Turns out the Bigwigs liked the sly way I slowly smiled, like I had a secret. They liked it so much, they wanted me to repeat it, even showing me the video to remind me what I'd done. No one had ever shown me my audition before so I was excited. I smiled onscreen and they pointed, "There, do that!" It was before I had the tips of my fangs sanded down a notch, my only attempt at remaking my beauty, and I'd smiled that way to cover the fang tips out of insecurity. You can't know what you're getting right any more than you can avoid looking like someone's ex that they hate, but if you're at an audition, you have a shot of getting the job. If you're at the callback, at least one person in the room thinks you might be the one the Bigwigs are looking for.

Keep Your Knees Bent

You have to be ready for anything at any time to truly take advantage of the opportunities that come your way. In many sports, you have to be ready for the ball at any moment, ready to score when it comes your way. You gotta keep your knees bent.

Make sure you have a passport and that it's up to date. Due to global unrest, there are times when it can take months to get a passport. Don't lose out on a great job in Japan because you didn't think ahead. Show business can include travel at a moment's notice. Be ready for it. Own a suitcase. If you have a pet, know a friend or kennel where you could take them or who'd be willing to watch them with very little notice. Until they can help with the rent, your dog can't be the reason you turn something down.

If you want your career to include action hero parts, learn to fight and fire a weapon. Faking can often be enough so you needn't get black belts to be able to fight like a pro on film, but it doesn't hurt to have a few moves in your pocket. Driving a car and riding a horse are also handy skills. Be ready for anything, especially the types of parts you'd like to play.

Wardrobe

In most cases, you are not expected to costume up for an audition. The occasional commercial may ask for a doctor's coat or waiter's uniform, but the Bigwigs don't expect you to have these things in your closet. The idea is that if you actually have something that looks like a police uniform or whatever, great, but they will supply you with one on the day. You only need to suggest the idea of the uniform for the audition. At the very least, don't get in the way of the Bigwigs being able to picture you in the costume of a police officer by wearing a floral sundress or a full beard.

As I said, you will usually be given a generic description of your character or none at all. The most common wardrobe description for most commercials is, "nice casual." This also works for most parts that lack description. Nice casual means different things for different types and age ranges but the general idea is to look put together in a non-distracting way. Before the Internet, the best way to judge what to wear was by watching TV. Wear to commercial auditions what people in your age and category wear IN commercials. Wear to TV auditions what people on that show wear. If you're auditioning for a detective in a new police drama, look at the characters on *CSI* or *Law and Order.*

I also find it helpful to buy my wardrobe after shooting. Not all sets allow it, but many are happy to offload their wardrobe at a pretty deep discount. These clothes have been selected by professionals for a job you booked. I own an entire wardrobe for a woman I've never been. She's a suburban woman with children. She wears cardigans, khaki pants and loafers or Keds. I also own several business suits that have never seen the inside of an office building. For awhile, I even had a white semi-formal sundress for all the brides I auditioned to play. Just like a uniform, most of these clothes don't feel like the "real" me, but I consider it part of my job to have my uniforms ready. If you're playing a colorful character, it may be helpful to make a very specific offbeat wardrobe choice. Just make sure it adds to the character rather than distracting from the audition. You don't need a puffy wedding gown when a feminine sundress will do. When I met with Quentin Tarantino about playing Lara Lee in *Django Unchained*, I didn't wear hoop skirts and carry a parasol. I wore a skirt and top that suggested the silhouette of a corset and hoops but were appropriate for modern street wear.

Men sit on a double-edged sword. Though they rarely need to carry more than a blazer and tie in their trunk to be ready for anything, when they are asked to wear a suit, they need to wear a suit, not the suggestion of one. Make sure you have at least one suit and that it fits well. Tailoring may cost a little, but what's fifty bucks if you look like a million?

A word on body image. Sometimes you will be asked to audition in a bathing suit or some other revealing garb. It is not your job to decide whether or not your body is "good enough" for the part. With 10 years of modeling experience and twenty of acting, I can assure you, the Bigwigs will do that for you. Your job is to select the most flattering swimsuit and wear it like you own it. It's therefore best if you think ahead for swimwear and other items that may be hard to shop for. Don't put yourself in a position to fail by shopping out-of-season at the only store selling suits then settle for the wrong size or color or silhouette. Even my friend who is over 300 pounds has done several parts in her underwear and a nude job on a hit cable TV show. You never know what call you're going to get or when. Keep your knees bent.

As a general rule, avoid red, white and black. Red reacts strangely to cameras and can appear orange or pink. White next to the face tends to turn eye-whites and teeth slightly yellow. Black tends to hide body definition. This is especially troubling if you thought your we're showing off your six-pack or your curves. Also, avoid turtlenecks as they can create the look of a floating head depending on the background. Avoid sheer. If you're not sure if something is sheer, photograph or videotape yourself to check. I find it helpful once in awhile to go through some of my wardrobe with a friend. Though tastes may differ, a friend can let you know if something is just not flattering or if it distracts from you.

When you get a callback, the Bigwigs are looking for more of the same so wear the same outfit. Postpone haircuts and shaving your beard. Remember, you may be the one who looks so right for the part that they're willing to overlook other flaws. Sometimes you may even be asked to wear your own outfit when they shoot. I find it useful to write down my wardrobe choices in my date book or on my script so I don't forget what I wore. I once had a callback 3 months after the first audition. I had no clue what I wore and have written notes down ever since. I recently got sloppy with this and found myself having to ask an actor I'd run into in the waiting room if he could remember what I was wearing. We both agreed on black pants but that's all we had. The last thing that should have been on my mind as I walked into that callback was, "Is this what I was wearing?" I focused and the director offered me the part, but it was a foolish mistake to have left something so simple to chance.

Props

I find it best to limit props to simple items you might normally have on you. A cell phone can be used as a prop phone, a remote control, a walkie talkie, a detonator, even a microphone. The palm of your hand can be a mirror. Your sides can be curtains or a door you push aside. They can also be files or photos. Be careful adding anything you wouldn't normally have on your person. It's fine to use your jacket as a blanket or to put a scarf on as your character is getting ready to go outside. It's potentially distracting to pull a frying pan and spatula out of your bag. It's downright upsetting to pull a bong, gun, hammer or knife from your jacket. Chances are, you'll be asked to stop, maybe even leave. Props are supposed to add to the reality of the scene, not put the Bigwigs in an awkward position. Anything you can live without is better left at home. As with your wardrobe choices, the idea is that any props would enhance your performance rather than distract from it.

Leave it at the Door

Whether you're wearing two different shoes, your hair got rained on, you got in an argument in the parking lot, shared the elevator with your ex, didn't get the sides in time, had the wrong address or whatever, leave it at the door. No one cares. Be a professional.

And, though you should have spent time preparing, working out all the beats, coming up with the perfect moves and great ideas, you kinda have to leave that at the door too. You may need to know if your character is an only child or a virgin but, the Bigwigs might not care. Backstory doesn't always make its way into a scene in any direct way. Think about how you deal with your own "backstory." Do you indicate that you're divorced while working at your computer? Do you "act out" that you have a twin while you're shopping for groceries? Surviving a car accident may be a defining moment for you, but you probably don't bring it up in conversation much. We all have our backstories but we don't walk around sharing slideshows and diaries. The martini-receiving Host may never know if Waiter has a college education or a dying sister or a gambling debt, but you should.

Perhaps you worked out some blocking for your scene. You may have to leave that at the door too. Maybe the room is smaller than you planned for or there's a wandering dog (seriously). Maybe the room is fine but the shot is only of your face and shoulders and you had planned to move around. No matter what you find in the room, you have to roll with it. You may find yourself having to leave your actions, your props and your backstory at the door. It'll be in good company next to your fears, insecurities, frustrations and excuses. All you really need in the room with you is a fully prepared original take and a willingness to roll with the punches. Things may not go as you planned so you have to prepare yourself to go with whatever happens and turn it into a win for you.

Own your Space

We're all Marlon Brando and Meryl Streep in our living room, but the minute you get to an audition, everything changes. You can't control who's in the waiting room or what tricks they may be willing to try to rock your concentration. You can't control whether you have to wait an hour and you have another audition to get to across town. Whether you had to overcome a flat tire, sitting in a room full of people more famous than you or finding out you're wearing the wrong outfit, the show must go on. There's no point in being there at all if you're not going to give it your all once it's your turn.

One way to leave everything at the door and make the best of your opportunities is to own your space. Though it's also very important to create the environment your character is experiencing, I'm talking about a point of view. Owning your space is about taking some control of the audition from the minute you walk in the door. Sometimes things won't go as you planned. You walk in to find a chair when you'd planned to do the audition standing or vice versa. Rather than freaking out, remember that you are a professional, able to take any direction and make it your own. You are prepared. If the direction is that you will be doing the audition seated, adjust. Take a breath if you need a minute to regroup, but let it go and get to work. Focusing on how things aren't going well will surely spiral into more things not going well. Anything you pay attention to will draw the attention of the Bigwigs. If you focus on the negative, so will they. If you remain unsinkable and adaptable, Bigwigs are free to focus on the positive.

I was once called for an audition with less than an hour to go home, print my sides, put on makeup, dress and drive to the audition. I was going straight to producers I'd never met before. Though the sides were only 4 pages, to my dismay and delight, the scenes were two very lengthy monologues. One monologue was confessing that I had cancer and needed help getting a plot at the National Cemetery.

The other was about being filled with exuberance and optimism after finding that I had been misdiagnosed. The second monologue was described as "rapid fire" and "breathy." Okay, so I not only had to read two long monologues about dying and not dying of cancer, I had to do one of them super-fast.

"Luckily," I'd had cancer removed years before and was able to tap into that experience as my backstory. I quickly filled in details and substitutions. I was once a military wife and had actually attended a funeral at the National Cemetery as a kid so I had good visual details. But there was no way to cram all those words into my head. I'd taken Margie Haber's classes on cold reading and found her technique of "dipping" invaluable. I drew lines on the script to separate ideas and sentence beats. I broke down what I wanted from the other person in each beat. While doing the first monologue, I said the first few words of a line then "dipped" my eyes down to pick up the rest of the sentence. If I got lost, I filled the moment with asking myself questions like, "Who am I talking to?" and "What do I want?" while lowering my eyes and searching the sides for the next line.

For the second monologue, I was still able to use "dipping," but it wasn't going to play well for me to luxuriate in searching my sides for cues. I thought about the major beats of the monologue, took a deep breath, started with the opening line in my head and dove in. Rather than worrying about the lines, I just spoke as quickly as I could, making it all up as I went and throwing in all the lines I could remember. It all happened so fast but I did notice the Bigwigs were laughing–a lot. Afterward, I called my manager and told her that they were either laughing because they thought I was delightful or they were laughing because they couldn't believe the audacity of someone coming in and spewing 2 solid minutes of talking without bothering to memorize any of the lines. I booked the job that day and continue to be proud of the work I did the next day on *JAG*. Yes, the next day. You gotta keep your knees bent. You have to be ready for anything at any time to truly take advantage of the opportunities that come your way.

It would have been easy to invest in the many excuses I could have made for sucking at that audition. I could have thrown in the towel before I even got there. Instead, I worked as quickly as I could, applying lipstick and memorizing lines at red lights while driving there. I broke down my script in the waiting room and figured out my take on the material. Instead of walking into the room with excuses and insecurities, I made a joke about hoping they were aware that I'd just received the material because it was about to become painfully evident. Then I settled in, created an environment for myself and set about being myself in the script's circumstances.

If you've done the work of at least understanding the scene and developing a unique take on the material, you have a shot at getting the job. Believe it could happen, no matter how unprepared you feel. You can't control that you only had an hour, but you can control your attitude. Maybe the odds are against you and everything really has gone wrong, but you have their attention and it's up to you where you focus that attention. Do the work, own your space, deliver and believe you just might pull it off.

Chapter 5:

Playing the Part

Arriving on Set

For those of you who are starting out, walking on a set can be overwhelming. Even if you're a working actor you can go months between jobs, even years. I'll admit that I can forget pretty basic things so I've tried to remember every question that's ever come up about what to do when you get to work. You have enough to worry about without getting thrown by a lost phone or shoes that hurt.

Generally speaking, someone will call you and confirm that you've received a call time and address. You usually have to park further away from "base camp," where the trailers are, or the set where you will be shooting. Often, you have to take a van from your parking spot to base camp so give yourself an extra 10-15 minutes to arrive. Production will provide breakfast (first meal) if you're arriving when the shooting day begins, but arrive even earlier if you want to get it yourself and have time to eat it. Otherwise, someone will bring it to you (usually the way you ordered but you never know until it arrives) and you will have to set it aside for make-up and risk it being hair-sprayed.

When you get to base camp, find anyone and ask them where to check in. You should have the name you'll be checking in with by now but you'll find almost everyone helpful on this question. If you can't find anyone, find the hair and make-up trailer and let them know you haven't checked in yet.

In your trailer, you should find a contract. Check the spelling of your name, your social security number and the address for your check. Show any corrections to the person who collects the contract from you. I still skim every piece of paper I sign and I read every word of any document I've never signed before. I also call my agent about documents I've never seen before to clear that I should sign them. Make sure you bring proper identification. If you're working as a local hire in a secondary market, also bring proof of residency. In your trailer, you should also find your "minis." Minis are the call sheet and the pages from the script that will be shot that day all shrunken down to about 5x8. Read through the pages to see exactly what you'll be doing that day and if any changes have been made to the script.

Don't get dressed until someone tells you. You may find your wardrobe hanging in your trailer when you enter, but you can't know how long it will be before they plan to use you. I was once on a movie for almost 2 weeks and only reported to set 3 times. Everyday, I'd arrive early, get my hair and make-up done and check my wardrobe to make sure it was all there. Then I'd sit on my stoop or hang out with the security guard or listen to one of the stars teaching himself ukulele for an upcoming role. I'd eat, read and crochet. I even made a real friend. Then I'd go home and prepare to do it again the next day. Edward G. Robinson once said, "The sitting around on the set is awful. But I always figure that's what they pay me for. The acting I do for free." Amen, brother. Point is, don't get dressed until someone tells you to and ask if you're not sure.

Wear shirts that are easy to remove. You may have your hair and make-up done while you're in your street clothes so don't wear a turtleneck. I try to wear shirts that can be unbuttoned or that have wide necklines. I know a lot of people like to wear sweats or other casual wear. I consider acting my job so I dress for work. Whether it's a sundress, a casual top and skirt, or jeans and a sweater, I try to make an effort to look good while staying comfortable. I enjoy expressing myself, my love of glamour, and the history of Hollywood. When I worked with Sam Raimi, even when he wore jeans and a t-shirt with sneakers, he wore a *Reservoir Dogs*-type jacket. I complimented him on it and he said he liked to dress for work and, like me, he enjoyed the glamour and history of this industry and didn't want to dress like he was going to the gym. Wear what you want to, but remember you are at work.

You can expect to be fed every 6 hours and there's always snacks at the craft service table, but I bring a protein bar or some nuts–just in case. Sodas aren't usually available for the first hour or more so bring your own if you're not a coffee drinker. Though production often provides them, I also bring slippers if I'm going to be wearing uncomfortable shoes. I always bring gel insoles for my shoes. Wardrobe should have moleskin if your shoes rub.

When you report to set, leave your cell phone in your trailer. You are working and are, therefore, unavailable. You are being paid for your time and attention. Some sets demand that you leave your phone in your car, especially if they don't allow photos. Plan ahead because no one but you cares about your phone.

If you wander off for any reason, be sure to let an A.D. know before you disappear. Things can change in an instant. Someone may tell you they won't be getting to you for hours then find the scene order has been flipped and you're up next. Keep your knees bent. You don't have to spend the day sitting in your trailer looking at your lines, but be ready to work at any time.

At the end of the day, make sure you sign out. Check that you aren't accidentally leaving with watches, jewelry or hair accessories. Unless you've been told otherwise, don't leave any personal items in the trailer overnight.

On Set Basics

If you have lines, you are part of the "first team." You may have a "stand-in" whose job is to look like you and stand in your spot for lighting and camera set-ups. It's a nice gesture to introduce yourself to your stand-in and stunt double, if you have one. While we were filming *Fantasy Island* Lauren Holly introduced herself to every background actor with which she had business. Now, I try to remember to do that also.

You will usually be given "marks;" tape, sandbags or tiny dot stickers, etc. placed where your feet should be. You may have a number of marks you have to hit in one scene. Unlike theatre, where being stage left might be enough, camera marks are precise. The camera and lights are set for those marks and those marks only. Even shifting your weight can change everything. If you can see the camera, the camera can see you. If you're not sure, close one eye to check if you can see the camera then repeat with the other eye. If you can't see the camera, adjust. If you feel light on your face, you're probably in the light. If not, adjust. If you notice that you are casting a shadow on your co-star, adjust. If you have any questions about whether you're doing it right, clarify during rehearsal.

Anything you put down on the set will be moved. Water bottles, purses, phones, books, knitting, scripts, etc, are all up for grabs. Many people will offer to keep an eye on things for you, but trust me when I say that their first order of business is not looking after your sweater. Unless you have your own cast chair, I suggest that you bring nothing to the set. You are working when you are on set. Even if you sit around for hours, you are at work. The employees of fast food places are capable of getting through a day without their iPad and so can you. It's fine to bring all those things to your trailer and use them while you're hanging around at base camp, but once you're on set, your attention should be focused on the work at hand. It doesn't matter if the star is playing with a toy, they have assistants to watch their things and personalized chairs with pouches to hold their things. You have work to do and only one shot at doing it well. Focus. Sometimes you want to bring a photo or a song with you or some other stimulus to help you access an emotional truth. In this era of cheap technology, I copy all photos and never bring originals. If I need a song, I bring an iPod Shuffle or some other easily replaced, inexpensive device and I label it with my name. Unless I can carry it on my body, I do not bring anything on set I can't afford to lose emotionally or financially.

Once you are mic'ed, consider your mic live. If you have to go to the bathroom, you may want to ask someone to disconnect your mic pack. No matter how uncomfortable the mic pack feels or how inconveniently the battery is located, you will forget you are wearing it. The advice I gave earlier about not engaging in negative conversations is critical on set. Not only can you be overheard or judge poorly with whom to share your thoughts, you could actually be talking about a person who's listening. Many people could be hearing you when you are mic'ed including the sound and camera crews, the director and producers. It is customary for people to share headphones with people from different departments or even guests on the set. If you are mic'ed, assume people can hear you. Keep your complaints and gossip to yourself. And be careful about exposing personal information, yours or someone else's. Cover your mic if you run into someone from AA or jail.

Take stunts seriously. If you're not comfortable with the stunts, let your double handle them. The more stunts you do yourself, the easier it is to edit the footage, but you don't have to dare yourself to do things you fear might injure you. Ask someone to show you what to expect and listen carefully to the instructions. I personally love doing my own stunts, but I also loved diving for volleyballs and competing in gymnastics after walking into the gym on crutches back in high school.

It is normal to shoot, or "cover" a scene from several directions. The bigger the budget, the more coverage you're likely to shoot. Typically, there's a "master" shot that covers everyone in the shot. There may be 2-shots (shots of you and one other person) and close-ups. Sometimes there are "insert" shots. Inserts may include shots of your hands doing something or some detail of your wardrobe, maybe even a product. These shots are often details described in the script so plan accordingly. If the script says, "He dials the phone," make sure your hands and nails are clean and camera-ready in case production needs an insert of you dialing.

The more coverage there is, the more chances you have to create a moment. Much of coverage will not be with the camera on you. If they shoot you last, try to use your co-stars' close-ups and on-camera time to rehearse your own choices off-camera. The more coverage you shoot, the longer your days may be, but the better your chances are of not ending up on the cutting room floor.

The days really can be very long. It is not unusual to have to wake super-early then work 12-16 hour days. But you can NEVER be the reason the day is long. Know your part and deliver. Listen carefully to instructions and direction. Be ready for anything.

All that said, sets can be a magical place. Though I couldn't find any confirmation of this number, there is general agreement that it takes about 200 people to make a movie happen. You can meet your future best friend or roommate or spouse on a set. You may watch others fall in love, even get married. Babies get born. You will celebrate birthdays and have inside jokes with people who you only just met. I've traveled the world for work and I've met amazing people, from billionaires to people who served time for manslaughter, that I would have never met any other way. While doing *Django Unchained*, many of us explored our family heritage and swapped stories of slaves and masters. We watched old movies from Quentin Tarantino's private collection every weekend with all the popcorn and candy we could eat and sometimes an introduction by Quentin or one of the actors. I've celebrated anniversaries, met newborns, played with dogs and learned new games on sets. Show business is a tough career but one of the upsides is getting to hang out on sets.

When you work outdoors, conditions can be extreme and physical discomfort can alter your experience. When you work indoors, you can lose all track of time and the outside world. If you're working out of town, you may battle homesickness or miss watching your child's first steps. But, you're all in it together on a set. People tend to try to make the best of things. Hesitate to judge when someone is cranky. You never know when was the last time they slept in their own bed, saw their children, had a long shower or got laundry done. Focus on your work and enjoy the magic of at least 200 people coming together to make something lasting.

Working with Cast and Crew

You are at work. Though this is a fun job and the environment can be very playful, making a movie, TV show or commercial is very expensive and the Bigwigs want to get what they paid for. Be yourself and enjoy yourself but remember this isn't about you. The electricians aren't given thirteen takes to get it right. Everyone has important work to do with people counting on them to get it done. Worry about yourself and focus on doing good work because film is forever. Rather than focusing on the size of your trailer or how uncomfortable your wig is, focus on making the most of the opportunity you've been given. This is your opportunity to do what you love for money and the opportunity to do work you can be proud of for decades to come.

Remember that the Bigwigs chose the wardrobe people just like they chose you, because they thought those people were the best for the job. Though you can bring your input to wardrobe, hair and make-up, you have to believe that the team, usually hired before you, has already spoken to the director and they have some idea of what the director wants. Both men and women can have adverse reactions to the hair, make-up and wardrobe choices. When men are just starting out, they may not be used to mascara or hairspray so it may look "wrong" to them. Women are often so used to doing their own hair and makeup that they have a certain way they like it, a certain way they feel "pretty." When Shirley MacLaine was reprising her *Terms of Endearment* role as "Aurora" in *The Evening Star*, she was reportedly "difficult." Difficult is a word often used to describe actors who know what they want and lack flexibility about their decisions. In the case of MacLaine, there's little chance anyone involved in that film had thought more about what Aurora would wear than Shirley had. If it's true she was "difficult," she seems entitled. She had already won an Academy Award and Golden Globe for the *Terms of Endearment* role more than a decade before.

You, on the other hand, are a hired gun. You are likely not the reason the movie got its financing or the person the Bigwigs hope will guarantee ticket sales in the millions. Odds are you're not playing a part you've had that much time to think about. You are probably not the only authority on what your character looks like. If you're not Shirley MacLaine reprising an award-winning part, maybe you're not the best judge of whether your make-up is "right" or your costume fits your character's taste. I have found it's better to ere on the side of trusting the hired experts. I've had makeup artists cover my skin in pancake and others have used nothing but moisturizer to smooth my complexion. Both looked "wrong" to me in the mirror. Both looked beautiful under the lighting. I was surprised to find that my hair can appear red, brunette or blonde in addition to its natural, unprocessed strawberry blonde. If I don't even know what color my hair will be until I see it on film, I have to admit I'm no expert on my own hair. Different camera lenses, film stocks and lighting setups can result in different textures and colors. Unless you're an expert in film makeup, let the director be the one to have an opinion of whether you look "right."

After your hair and make-up are done and you have been seen by the director, consider it your job to arrive on set looking just that way–even if you hate the look or it takes hours to get to your scene. I take this so seriously that I hold myself responsible for not touching my face or hair throughout the day. If I found an unplugged extension cord on set, I would notify someone rather than touching it myself. Just like the lighting and sound crew, hair and make-up artists are usually union professionals so I take falling barrettes and mascara smears to the trailer for touch-ups. I use straws to avoid disturbing my lipstick. They're usually available at craft services and some makeup artists have them. I use Q-tips if I need to wipe a tear or get something out of my eye. Perhaps this all seems silly to you, but my guess is that you don't enjoy having people constantly touching your face and hair. If so, then consider this advice on how to avoid being messed-with after you get out of the chair. Remember, it's not your hair and make-up, it's your character's hair and make-up. It's not your job to like it, it's your job to own it.

If you've avoided putting on your wardrobe until someone tells you to, you may still have to sit around in a tuxedo for hours. I make a concerted effort to avoid wrinkling jackets, skirts or slacks while waiting around. If you have to eat in your wardrobe, tuck napkins into your collar and cover your lap. You may look like a 3 year old with a mother who hates laundry, but if you're on sets often enough, you'll get used to seeing people with giant rollers in their hair or other humiliations. Remain unstained.

Sometimes respect turns to gratitude. I know actors who give presents to hair and makeup or other people they couldn't have done without. I've also had grateful crew members reward me with gifts. Don't spend more than you can afford as a thoughtful gift is always more memorable. Even a heartfelt card can make someone's day. The longer you work with people, the more likely this activity is, but it is by no means a requirement. To thine own self be true.

When I worked on *Friends*, the cast had just recently banded together in solidarity to receive equal pay raises. It was the 22nd episode of their third season and the writers, producers, cast and crew were a well-oiled machine. The other guest stars on the episode were Jon Favreau, Dina Meyer and Ben Stiller. The director, Peter Bonerz ("Jerry" the dentist on *The Bob Newhart Show*) was shooting his seventh episode with the series. I was replaceable, new to acting on-camera and the stranger on set. Walking into a situation like that, I learned that you have to assume that each take is your last. If the director and the stars are happy with the take, you're "moving on."

When I worked with Sammo Hung on *Martial Law*, his English was labored. If he got all the words right and in the right order, that was the take. My most emotional scene was a walking shot in a dog park. Even with hitting our marks and ignoring dogs, I was able to play the scene honestly and fully several times. Then I had a take where I knew I had "pushed" the emotion. I was acting, not being in the moment. Sammo Hung got every word right that time and we were "moving on." I mentioned to the director that I felt I had another take in me, that I was concerned that I had pushed. He was happy and already thinking of the next shot. The Acting Police are still looking for me for that one. It can be humbling to know which one you are when the answer is "replaceable" "new" and "stranger," but it can also be empowering. Since I am aware that there are more important things happening on the set than my performance and that my performance is most important to me, I can focus on creating a moment. On some sets there may be so many stars who aren't interested in the director's input that the director will focus all their energy (and perhaps frustration) on you, but on most sets, you will be in charge of your own choices and delivery.

As with the other departments, I try to respect the job of continuity. I avoid elaborate movements and gestures unless they are worth the effort. I avoid interacting with a bunch of props that require a lot of resetting unless they are worth the effort. Check first if you want to consume any of the food or beverages on the set or light a cigarette or break something.

I also try to keep the sound crew in mind. Whether you zip your jacket, run water in a sink or chew food, the sound department may have trouble getting clean takes. If the sound isn't good, takes can be wasted or you may have to "loop" the scene later. Looping is recording the dialogue later (often months later) in a room with nothing but a mic and your scene on a screen. Though looping can be an opportunity to fix things, it's usually difficult to do well and can affect your performance adversely, so I endeavor to avoid it. If you think it was hard to get a moment right with all the actors and props around, wait until it's just you and some headphones giving you a three-beep cue.

In general, remember that you are the one the Bigwigs chose for the part, the one they are counting on to deliver, but you are also a small cog in an expensive 200 person machine. If you need to feel "important," just walk by the background holding area. Any one of those people would gladly take your place, no matter how "wrong" your hair looks or how many of your lines got cut.

If your part is big enough, your agent powerful enough and/or the budget big enough, you may have a full-sized trailer with a gift basket inside. I'll admit it's fun to have a big trailer and some of the gifts can be pretty cool, but I try to focus on what's really at stake– the stuff that ends up on film. No one in the audience will know or care that you had to share a honey wagon so why should you? It's true that perks can be an indication that you've become a big shot, but they won't help you nail a character or steal a scene.

As I stated before, some directors will work closely with you, but most will expect you to come in and deliver on your audition's promise whether they direct you or not. Some actors are generous in sharing the limelight and some are generous with helping you do a good job. Lauren Holly literally tugged at my pants pocket out of the camera's sight to help me hit a long series of marks in a tracking shot. Others won't speak to you and may even leave when it's time for your close-ups. It is your job to act with the person reading the script off-camera or stare lovingly at the tennis ball on the C-stand (a pole usually used for lighting) beside the camera. The show must go on and it's finally your chance to shine. Don't let your personal feelings, insecurities and rejections get in the way of your moment. Focus.

Sometimes you get lucky enough to work with a director or actors who are open to your suggestions. Pick your moments wisely if you think you have a great idea. If your idea doesn't change the meaning of the scene, go ahead and try it without asking. Ask forgiveness, not permission. But, if your idea would change the story or the dialogue AND you feel like the director or actor is open to ideas, it's best to offer it as an idea before allowing the director to burn film. I've found that, before "moving on," if everyone seems happy with what's been filmed but you still have an idea, you can ask the director if it's "in the can," meaning that they're satisfied they have the shot, then offer your idea and ask for another take. Sometimes the fact that you've delivered helps build confidence that your ideas may be worth listening to or even trying. Generally speaking, the more experienced and known you are, the more freedom you will have to try things.

You are not the crew so don't concern yourself too much with their jobs. Focus on creating an unforgettable moment no matter what the gaffer is doing, where the lighting flags are placed or whether you got a gift basket. You are not the star, so focus on doing your best to rise to the occasion and don't worry about perks or entourages.

No matter how big a name you are, there are times when you jump into a project that's been up and running for some time. If you're guest starring on a TV show, that cast and crew may have been working together on that set for 8 years. The cast's dressing rooms may be like a home away from home. Even if you're joining a film that's been shooting for a couple of months, certain things will already be in place when you arrive. People will have routines and relationships and private jokes. Think of it like jumping rope. Try to get up to speed as quickly as possible and don't stop the rope by trying to fit in too soon. Take friendship where it's offered but worry more about your work than whether you get to sit at "the cool table" at lunch.

Rehearsals

Most of the time, you will be given a rehearsal before rolling. Before you get too excited about discussing you character with Soderbergh, most of these rehearsals are for camera and sound blocking and various other departments. That said, you can still make the most of a rehearsal, even if you're off-camera. Though stars may opt to have someone else do their off-camera work, most actors are not afforded this option. I actually prefer to be off-camera first as it gives me an opportunity to practice and explore ideas before trying them in front of the camera. Let's face it, I don't find work everyday. I can get rusty. Rehearsal gives me a chance to settle in and work out the kinks.

Always be open to a better idea. Sometimes it's worth explaining your ideas when you get an adjustment from a director, but it's usually best to take the adjustment and make it work. You don't have the whole movie in your head, the director does. The director has been thinking about this scene long before you even knew it existed. Even if you think the director is wrong and you've stated your case reasonably, you still have to fully commit to their idea and deliver. Especially during the rehearsal process, let the director try things with you. It's okay to disagree with your director about your character, but if you want to stay off that cutting room floor, you'll try to deliver at least the performance the director expected when they hired you.

Improvisation, Ad-libbing and Surprises

Some directors, particularly those who didn't write the script, are open to improv, ad-libbing and surprises. In the theatre world, we are trained to say every single word as written, but in film and TV, there can be a lot more room for collaboration. During the audition process, I try to stick to the script unless the script indicates a place for ad-libs, like, "Lara Lee holds court." By the time I reach the set and know my character better, I may want to add or change some piece of dialogue. Pay attention. Are other actors improvising? Is the director reacting well to it? If you ad-libbed well during the audition, perhaps they hoped you'd bring your ideas to the scenes.

If something goes wrong during the scene, you are expected to do or say what you can to keep the scene going until someone yells, "Cut." Things "going wrong" can actually be a great opportunity to shine by staying in the moment and saving the situation. Movies are filled with magical moments that weren't planned. The day of the big sword fight in *Raiders of the Lost Ark*, Harrison Ford was sick so Indiana Jones just shot the sword wielder instead. It's a great and funny surprise that endears Jones to us.

Always be ready to improvise actions. Most of the time, we don't get much time to explore a set and its props before we shoot. Even so, we are called upon to interact with a set and its props, sometimes like it's a place we know like the back of our hand. If the script mentioned actions, maybe you had time to come up with some ideas but, until you get on the set, it's hard to know if those ideas will work. The cinematographer and director haven't seen you in the set until you arrive to work. They may come with new ideas once they see you in context. Keep your knees bent. If you've broken down the scene and practiced, you should have plenty of ideas about how your character does things, no matter what you are asked to do.

In addition to your director's ideas, your fellow actors will have come up with a few ideas of their own. Some actors will show you what they have in mind or discuss ideas during rehearsal. Other actors like to keep everything alive by holding some things back until the camera rolls. Still others honestly don't know what they're going to do until it happens. Whatever happens, keep going. Remember, only the director can stop a scene. I've been goosed, kissed and grabbed without warning but I try to react in the context of the character and the scene. While filming *Pretty Woman,* Richard Gere jokingly snapped the jewelry box lid down on Julia Roberts' hand as she reached for the necklace. Julia's laugh was so genuine, the moment made the final cut and was even used in the trailer.

Sometimes technical surprises occur. I'm not going to tell you to ride out an earthquake with lights falling around you or curtains catching fire, but short of that, keep going until you hear, "Cut." Movies are filled with punches that accidentally landed and other real-life injuries. The show must go on. The cuts and bruises will go away but film is forever. Expect the unexpected. There's an old saying that there are three movies, the one in the script, the one you shoot and the one the editor sculpts. I would argue that there is a fourth movie, the one life makes. Call it God or nature or fate, but there are things that happen that shape movies and are not controlled by you, the writer, the director, or the editor. The director may have cast River Phoenix in *Interview with the Vampire*, but fate cast Christian Slater. An entire island sunk when a storm hit the set of *Waterworld*. Sometimes a star is delayed by a previous project or has to leave early for their next gig which can affect the entire shooting schedule. Sets catch fire, women get pregnant, people get injured, shit happens. That said, I've found that these curve balls can have a positive affect on the movie, even if they throw the set into turmoil. When I was shooting one of my short films, I had secured two locations, one for each of our 2 shooting days. As I was gearing up to shoot, I lost the first location with about 24 hours notice. As we prepared for the next day of shooting, we once again lost our location with 24 hours notice. In both cases, I ended up with far better locations. Movie making is problem solving. When things seem to be spinning out of control, it could be because life often directs its own version of the movie. I'm not saying it will always be changes for the better, I am saying get used to it.

When it All Goes Wrong

Life is not fair. I worked on *Hell Ride* for 7 years getting it ready for production. On the day of my biggest dialogue scene, the only scene to make the cut, I woke up with laryngitis. It was disheartening, to say the least. I had to let go of my fantasy of how that day would go and focus on finding my voice. I spent the day drinking honeyed tea and taking holistic remedies. Though I was wearing a catsuit with a mic cord running from my bra to my boot making the bathroom an ordeal, I had to keep pumping fluids until I looked several months pregnant. When it came time to film, it didn't go the way I planned, it went better. Michael Phillips of the Chicago Tribune wrote, "And in a bit role as a bartender, Laura Cayouette intones the line 'You must be ... The Gent' in a voice so sultry she's halfway to the post-coital cig as she's saying it. Her smile, however, suggests an actual actress having actual fun, in a movie where everyone around her is either hiding behind sunglasses or mud-wrestling." I delivered and my laryngitis came across as "sultry," not as an illness.

Every actor has gotten stuck on a line. You "go up" during the scene and everyone laughs it off. The next take, you blow the exact same line. Then you just get stuck on stupid, disrupting take after take. Someone says, "Take 23" and you die inside knowing it's all your fault. The good news is it really has happened on most sets and to most actors. Nobody's perfect and I've seen it happen to many seasoned pros. Try to stop and take a breath. Ask yourself questions. Who are you? Who are you talking to? What do you want from them? Focus on <u>why</u> you're talking and, hopefully, you'll get less tripped up by the words you are saying.

Sometimes a director or fellow actor will call you out on something publicly. Try to keep a sense of humor if you can. No matter what happens during work, only the film will last to tell the story. Don't let your personal feelings get in the way of doing great work. Focus on your character's feelings in the scene. If you want to play with the big boys, you may have to take some big hits. Just like in football or boxing, you're usually expected to take it in stride and focus on delivering. Sometimes you may feel the need to defend yourself. Remember that it's possible to defend your character choices without defending your ego. No one truly cares how <u>you</u> feel, they are trying to film what your character feels. Focus on that and try to avoid personality conflicts.

As if it weren't already tough enough to be great, you may find yourself the victim of sabotage. There are actors who feel the need to undermine others. Maybe they mess up your cues then blame you. Maybe they hide your props or suggest that your character not speak or be killed off. Maybe they even try to get you fired. Don't panic. Just because a star wants something doesn't mean they will get it and non-stars usually have limited power. Though it may break your heart to see how human your heroes and co-workers can be, it doesn't have to break your spirit. I try to remember that people have lots of insecurities and fears and some process their fears through aggression. I try to see it as flattering that anyone would see me as a threat. Above all, I do not let other people's behavior change my professionalism. I have found that the best defense against a saboteur is to deliver an amazing performance no matter what crap anyone pulls. I have also learned that the best way to prove someone is spinning is to remain very still. The more calm you are, the more obvious it becomes which one of you is acting out of desperation. At home, I let my frustrations and disappointments out, but on set I try to stay focused on the work. Filming usually doesn't last more that a few months but film is forever. If you can't let go of your frustration and disappointment on set, then endure it and focus on forever.

What You Wished For

No matter how long your days, how uncomfortable your costume or how rude your director, remember–you wanted this. The reason people tell you to be careful what you wish for is because sometimes you get it. For every time you feel exhausted, uncomfortable or frustrated, there are plenty of people wishing they'd gotten your part. Heck, you'd be one of them if you hadn't booked the gig. Acting can be a grueling job, but it's the job you wanted. There's an old joke about the allure of this industry. A guy has the job of cleaning up the elephant poop at the circus. Someone asks why he doesn't get a better job and he replies, "And leave show business?" No matter how small your part or how tough the work is, if you're on a set, you're in showbiz. Nothing else feels quite like it.

Acting is a job of hurry-up-and-wait. Even the biggest stars sit around waiting to work. No matter how big your part, you may be called upon to basically be background in scenes. Shirley MacLaine saw her opportunity to steal our scene in *The Evening Star* just as Philip Seymour Hoffman filled his moment in the background in *Boogie Nights*, but neither had any lines in those scenes. Maybe they were only in the scene for continuity, but they turned their minutes into moments. Attitude is a matter of perspective. Great actors are never "just background," they are fully alive people who aren't talking at that time.

Long days, physical discomfort and sitting around waiting can all affect your mood. This is the job. This is what you wished for. You may feel frustrated, maybe even disappointed, but just like any other profession, you can't let it get to you. Your character has their own feelings. Focus on those. If you still have time on your hands, try to focus on the positive. You got the part. You are on a set working with professionals. You are gaining experience. You are doing what you love and getting paid. When it all starts to get to me, I remind myself that there are people all over the country, sitting in cubicles or standing behind counters, wishing they loved their jobs.

Acting isn't for everyone. There are hundreds of auditions, most of which you won't get. Even Meryl Streep isn't "right" for every part. After stomaching the rejections long enough to find work again, the work can be tough physically and emotionally. On set, there are going to be moments that affect your ego, moments when you feel left out or insulted. You will spend hours waiting around for your moment. You will miss weddings and funerals only to find out you've been rescheduled for next week. But, that's the job. Like in the military, you may leave your home, or even the country, for months. Like athletes, you may have to perform physically demanding tasks over and over. You may even train for years for a skill no one ever films. Like doctors, you may have to be on-call or work all-nighters. You may have to cry on cue or live through being raped over and over. That's the job. If you wish to be an actor, then that's the job you're wishing for.

Chapter 6:

Commercials

Typecasting

A lot of commercial casting comes down to types. It's critical that you know your type and dress the part. Commercial casting is usually broken down first by age range. No matter your actual age, your look will have it's own age range category. Trust your agents to know your category unless you find you can't book or get callbacks in that category because you look older or younger than everyone else. Maybe you think of yourself as edgy but it might be worthwhile to cover your tattoos and see yourself in a new light. Maybe you look just right in a suit to everyone else, even if it feels like it's not "you."

If you're not sure which category you are, it can be helpful to ask friends, even strangers, for words that describe your look. Are you perceived as suburban, glamourous, sexy, hip, nerdy, athletic, tough, chic, professional, street, mechanical? Do you look like a mom, plumber, CEO, teacher, doctor, president, biker, prince charming, librarian, bouncer, college student? You might be surprised to find that people see you differently than you see yourself. There are certain categories that work more than others so it might be great if you think of yourself as a drummer but your friends see you as a dad type. You might be in your 30's and find that your friends perceive you as a college kid or someone middle aged. In commercial categories, perception is pretty much everything. Figure out the category that best fits your look and focus on that rather than how it makes you feel to wear a suit instead of surfer shorts.

Watch Commercials

In the age of TiVo and DVRs, it's important to note that the best preparation for commercial auditions is watching commercials. Notice which parts people in your category normally play. What are they wearing? Which products do they usually represent? What special skills do those people have? How do they make moments seem real or funny or heartfelt? The people who got those commercials have something to teach us about getting those jobs. It doesn't matter if you know the guy from class and he sucks, he got the job for a reason. Rather than detracting from his moment, try to figure out why he was chosen.

It's easier to accept when a job you went in for goes to someone far older, heavier, better looking or more famous than you. The time to look for answers within yourself is when someone your type gets the part. What choices did they make? Were they stronger than yours? Could you have done it the way they did it? Why didn't you? It may be that the reason you didn't get the job is something totally arbitrary like hair color or height, but it's not a bad idea to ask yourself whether you're making strong choices and to learn from others' successes. It doesn't matter if that guy in your class really does suck, he did something right and you might be able to learn from it.

Signing In and Size Cards

When you arrive at a commercial audition, you must first sign in. It's common at commercial auditions for you to fill out a size card, or at least it used to be. In L.A., most commercial casting places now require a bar code. You fill out your size card on a computer once and participating casting directors simply scan the barcode before your audition. Your bar code will pull up a photo, resumé and size card for the Bigwigs. In most other cities, you will be required to provide your headshot and resumé and fill out a size card.

Size cards ask for all kinds of information. Obviously, there's a heavy focus on your sizes and you would do well to know them. Some cards will even ask for your hat or glove size. If you don't know specifics, at least know if you're a small, medium or large.

Don't lie. If you want to fudge your weight a few pounds, maybe it won't matter, but if your feet are a size eight, not a seven, it could make for a long day. Wardrobe will usually call you for your sizes again if you book the job, but the sizes on the card are just information–not a confession. Take a deep breath and fill in the blanks.

However, I do not fill out my card in its entirety. For address, I give my zip code only. It lets the Bigwigs know I live in the area without telling anyone how to find me. I also leave any questions about age blank. It's illegal for the Bigwigs to ask your age (though they can ask if you're above 25 for liquor ads or other age-sensitive products), so you're under no obligation to fill in the age. The question is mostly meant for children anyway. I don't fill in my age range either. I figure the Bigwigs will make their own assumptions and I would rather not try to read their minds in advance.

Some size sheets ask about driving. This is mostly for background players but can appear on any size card. Some ask if you're willing to do background work. If you want to do background work, commercials pay well and tend to have short shooting days. If you don't want to be a background player, it can be wise to leave it blank. I was recently hired for a commercial but only if I would sign on as a background player the Bigwigs said they planned to upgrade. I'd never done background work on a commercial and felt a little humbled by it all, but I took a chance. I was treated like a principle all day and became optimistic about making the cut. Three months later, they cut me into two spots, a national and a wild spot, both as a principle. Me and my bank account are happy I took the chance.

Never use your social security number anywhere on your size card or on the sign in sheet. Memorize your SAG-AFTRA number and use this instead or simply write, "on file." In the age of identity theft and stalkers, it's best not to give more information than is necessary. I've never gotten in any trouble for the blanks I've left on size cards, but handing over my photo, phone number, address, email and other personal details all in one place could lead to trouble.

Size cards often ask for special skills. As a general rule, if you are fairly athletic or coordinated, say yes to any athletic skill asked of you. Don't dare yourself to do something that may injure you if you aren't proficient, like walking a tightrope or doing flips. But if you haven't been on a bike since high school, it's still okay to say you can ride a bike. Then, after the audition, find a bike and ride it. That way, even if you don't get the callback, you'll be ready and confident for next time.

Find the Story

There is usually a script, even if there are no lines. The script often describes the general storyline and any actions you will be asked to perform. Sometimes a copy of the "storyboards," the story of the commercial drawn out like a comic strip of the shots, will be posted. If so, study them for the general story and tone of the piece as well as activities. You've seen plenty of commercials and many share similarities, so it should be fairly easy to discern the tone from the storyboards.

Once you think you understand why the commercial is funny, revealing or romantic, etc., break down your objectives and substitutions for personal details like you would any other script. Who are you talking to and what do you want from them?

Never forget that the Bigwigs' objective is to sell a product. As such, everything about the product is positive. Unless specifically directed otherwise, you always have positive reactions to the product. The product is the solution to every problem and the happy ending to every story. For example, if you are asked to read straight into the camera, think of someone you would tell this story to, the story of how this aspirin substitute saved you from a migraine. Use a friend or relative, someone you're close to, then genuinely tell them the story. If it's meant to be funny, try to make your friend laugh. If it's heartfelt, try to get them to cry. Invest, don't sell. Tell the story like its your truth.

In the Room

When you first get in the audition room, there will be a simple lighting and camera set-up. If you have lines, they are often written on cue cards to the side of the camera. That said, its best to be as "off-book," or memorized, as possible for a commercial audition. If there are props, they will usually be supplied. Listen closely to any direction given. The Bigwigs may give you a long series of actions. Memorize them. If you don't think you have it, ask them to repeat it. Once. Then, just do your best to keep telling the story if you get lost during the take.

You will be asked to "slate." This means they want you to say your name into the camera. Sometimes you will also be asked to state your agency, your height or whether you can ride a bike or do some other special skill. Sometimes during a slate, you are asked to show your hands to the camera. It's a good idea for both men and women to keep their nails filed and clean. You may love your cherry nail polish, but the young mom choosing diapers in the spot probably doesn't sport cherry nails. Let your freak flag fly on your toenails instead.

Sometimes you are asked to give profiles. You don't have to turn your whole body, like in a mug shot, unless instructed to. Turn your head and shoulders to one side. Bring your eyes back to camera first and let your head follow. Repeat on the other side. Bringing your eyes back first can be the very thing that stops the Bigwigs from fast forwarding through you on the tape. If you don't believe in the power of this move, tape yourself doing the mug shot method, then the eyes first method, and see for yourself.

Remember that this is an opportunity and that everything about this product is positive. If you're not the smiling type, keep a pleasant look on your face during your slate. It's the first impression the Bigwigs have of you. Even if you're playing a cranky person in the spot, they want to see you as a positive addition to their set, someone pleasant to be around.

It is NEVER your job to cut a take. I once did a commercial with a movie star who, if she didn't like the take, would make it unusable by cursing or dropping something. But she was a movie star and even she never just quit a take before the director yelled cut. It's not your job to critique your work. You are not in charge of when the take is cut. Muscle through, no matter how badly it goes. If it all goes sideways, at least maintain a sense of good humor about it.

Auditions, especially commercial auditions, are like lottery tickets. The more you accumulate, the better your chances of winning. Better luck next time, if this wasn't your best day. Acting, and especially auditioning, is like hitting home runs. Mickey Mantle was the greatest at knocking it out of the park, but he almost always struck out. Shake it off and keep your knees bent for the next one.

Being "Real"

We've discussed testimonials, where you speak directly into the camera as if it were a friend, but there's another kind of being real. Many commercials today like to sell without directly addressing the consumer. They want the story to speak for itself and for the characters to be relatable. The Bigwigs want the audience to see themselves in the actors and solve their issues the way the characters do—by using the product.

In these spots, you are definitely playing a character, but they want it to be a heightened slice-of-life piece, where we feel it's all real. For actors who break down scenes, develop characters, choose interesting and high stakes objectives, substitute personal details and go for wins, these auditions are your moment to shine. Just remember, it's a 30 second spot for discount tires, not a scene from

Shakespeare. Do the work then let it go and be a real person in a real moment.

Humor

Funny is money. Commercial funny isn't always the same as ha-ha funny but some of the same general rules apply. The biggest difference between comedy and drama is how far a person is willing to go to win and what's at stake. In a drama, you may be willing to kill and that's pretty darn far, but in a comedy, people go to the ends of the earth just to get to a phone before it stops ringing. I remember an episode of *The Andy Griffith Show* where all Don Knotts' "Barney Fife" had to do was answer the phone right next to him. It turned into a three ring circus. The phone flipped and slipped, dangled and conked. I'm almost positive that the script read, "Barney answers the phone."

The key to comedy is committing. Purple shirts are especially unwelcome in comedy. Don't do anything halfway. In comedy, if something goes wrong in the scene, you have just become the lucky recipient of another obstacle. Obstacles are comedy gold. Barney bobbled the phone, got tangled in its cord and held it upside down before finally achieving the simple task of answering the phone (or at least, that's how I remember it). If you can figure out how to create a character, fully commit, tell a story and make people laugh, you will definitely work. There are quite a few talented actors who can convince us that a pain medication relieved their pain, but there are precious few who can make answering a phone funny.

Improv

Sometimes you'll be asked to improv. SAG-AFTRA has rules on improvising at auditions and those rules are good ones designed to protect you from having the Bigwigs use your lines in the spot without even notifying you, much less paying you. That said, I still improv lines at auditions knowing that I'm unprotected. There was only one instance I'm aware of where a commercial used my improved lines in the spot, but they hired me to say two of them. I got a kick out of knowing I'd come up with one of the lines someone else said in the spot.

It's good to take a class or two in improv, but as a general rule, keep everything positive. Sometimes you are asked to improv with someone else. You cannot control what your acting partner says. Disagreeing can shut down a train of thought and deaden the energy. It's okay to take something in a new direction or change the subject, but make sure you're adding something, not just squashing someone else's ideas. Go with the flow but don't let your acting partner walk all over you. It's good to have some ideas for specific actions and lines ready before you walk in the room. Be ready to abandon your ideas for better ones, but it's always good to have some ideas ready to save the day if the scene goes flat or gets too chatty. Being chatty may get you more attention, but it's better to have some solid, supportable ideas that land.

Be willing to be silly, play and have fun. Commercials are filled with big moments, grand gestures and flights of fancy. I went in for a spot where my husband and I had to pretend to sit on a couch reading and chatting until a football crashed through a window on our right and out another on our left. Then we had a line that didn't seem all that funny, but I could see from the tone that it was meant to be funny so I went with that. Afterward, I found out that the football was to be thrown by Saints Quarterback Drew Brees' 3 year old son. Suddenly, the whole spot made sense and was, in fact, pretty cute and funny. Assume that the Bigwigs know what they're doing and go with it.

Cattle Calls

Sometimes it will feel like the Bigwigs called in every actor in the state for a commercial audition. I've even been to callbacks with packed waiting rooms. It usually means they are looking for a type. Many commercials have no lines and require no more from your part than that you walk through a door or hand someone an ice cream cone. In this case, the Bigwigs are looking for a physical type, a look, more than anything else.

Often, when Bigwigs have to get through a lot of people quickly, they will call in many of you at one time. Sometimes they have you stand on a line side-by-side. Other times, they allow you to take turns. To get a sense of your personality, they may ask you all to do an activity (like the dreaded chicken dance) or, more often, answer a question. You usually don't know the question in advance but there are, as always, general rules.

Unless specifically asked, do not answer any questions by talking about your acting career. The answer to what you did last weekend is NOT "rehearsed for this great play I'm doing," or "took this great agent seminar." Even if that's the truth, pick a weekend recently when you visited your grandmother or took your dog to obedience school and tell that story. You can talk about something that happened at fencing class without ever mentioning that it's for a play you're doing.

The point of the question is to give you an opportunity to reveal yourself and give the Bigwigs some idea of your ease in front of a camera. The one thing the Bigwigs already know about you is that you're an actor. Commercials can require many special skills so the question is a good opportunity to show that you're well-rounded. The point is not to give you an opportunity to list what's on your resumé or your coming attractions. Try to give your answer highs and lows and all the natural expressions that go with them. If you tell a story, give it a beginning, middle and end. But keep it short. Commercials are short and the people who make them like to see that you understand what it takes to land a story effectively in a short period of time. It's not a bad idea to have a few stories at the ready. What's your most embarrassing moment? Tell us about a hobby. Where's your favorite place? Who would you most like to meet? And, of course, what did you do last weekend?

At a cattle call, it's imperative to stand out in a crowd, but it looks insecure or desperate to grab attention from anyone else. Let everyone have their turn. You can't know what the Bigwigs are looking for so keep your focus on yourself and the directions. It doesn't matter if the person next to you is taking too long or making fun of what you said, you have your turn and that's your opportunity to shine. Sometimes all you get to do is stand on a line holding a number (cattle calls sometimes have numbers or a sign with your name) and give your name and profiles. Be yourself, be pleasant and remember to use your moment to connect with the people watching by bringing your eyes forward first to draw their attention in. Hold their attention by being positive and well-rounded.

Remember the Product

The idea of most commercials is that the product improves life somehow. It is the point of the spot. Sometimes you are asked to interact with an actual product, an item. If the product is soup and you are asked to pick up the can, be sure any label is facing the camera. Without doing anything too unnatural, try not to obstruct the label much. Make sure you're holding the product high enough for the camera to see it.

Sometimes you're asked to eat at an audition. Bread or crackers are often substituted for the product. If the piece of bread is supposed to be a burger, hold it like a burger and enjoy it like a satisfying juicy burger, not a stale piece of white bread. Unless otherwise instructed, and especially if you have a line, it's best to take a small bite and chew it like a bigger one.

A word on shooting food scenes. Sometimes the food is cold or just plain awful. Too bad. That's why they call it acting. Unless otherwise instructed, all reactions to eating a product are positive. If you book the part, you may have to do dozens of takes while shooting so it's usually best to use the spit bag if it's provided. Of course, you will end up swallowing several bites of food, but you won't make yourself sick overeating.

In film and television, the story is the thing, but in commercials, the product is the story. Whether its a spot for insurance or light beer, commercials strive to illustrate their product's positive impact on life. Even if no part of the spot seems to reference the product, it all makes sense to the Bigwigs somehow. Your job is to help them illustrate their point.

Working

Most commercials shoot in less than a week. Many only need you for 1 day and the days tend to be shorter. Some actors get disappointed if they aren't featured or if they have no lines. Unlike film and TV where you want as much screen time as possible, in commercials, less is usually more. As long as you're "recognizable," you get paid the same. Unless you are a spokesperson, you may not want your face over-associated with a particular product. Other advertisers don't want people saying, "That's the Taco Bell guy" while they're watching the anti-depressant ad they just aired. I'm not suggesting that you hold back in any way, I'm just saying it's okay not to get a lot of camera-time in a commercial.

If you're working with a reputable agent, you should get checks and plenty of them, shortly after your spot starts to run. That said, it's always good to keep records of what time your spot runs, what channel it appears on and during which show. I even keep a record of other people's sitings. I once caught a station airing one of my commercials without permission–in Hawaii. You may never need this information, but it's better to have it and not need it than to need it and not have it.

There have been products I wasn't willing to represent. It's okay to have the occasional "sick day" for an audition once in awhile. If you're unwilling to do the ad, don't waste anyone's time with callbacks. Most importantly, be ready to defend your decision. Your agent has every right to be frustrated with you if your principles make you difficult to work with. Remember, your agency is just fine with booking that spot.

I've been lucky to have advertised many of my own favorite products. I've gotten to do spots that made people laugh and commercials people talked about. I've even traveled to Paris, Prague, San Francisco, the desert and the beach to shoot commercials. The best thing about commercials is you get to do what you love for money. Commercials are the gift that keeps on giving. Most only air from 3 weeks to 3 months, but some can run for years. Unless you're contract is regional or was for a "buyout," a spot where they pay you a one time fee and no residuals, you'll get paid every time it airs. Not bad for a day's work. Even if it's only financially, it's a great way to turn a minute into a moment.

THE BIZ

Chapter 7:

Making the Most of It

It's Show BUSINESS

Now that you have the tools to work, it's time to look at marketing tools and business basics. There are many reasons actors become one of the 1% of our union who are able to support themselves. There are as many ways to "make it" as there are people who've done it. Some people are well-connected. They're married to a network executive or their last name is Coppola. Some people are super-talented. Some make our hearts skip a beat or make us laugh a lot and we pay to see them again and again. But the ones who stick around understand that this is a business and there's a lot of money at stake.

As an actor, you are usually one of the lowest costs on the set. That can make you very replaceable. The good news is that it can also lead to a lot of overtime and golden time. As one of the lowest expenses, the Bigwigs are hoping you will be one of the lowest maintenance issues on the set as well. They expect you to be in charge of yourself. Don't wait until you're on a set to start doing this. Think of acting as a career and think of your career as a business. Jobs tend to have predictable incomes attached, but when you start a business, there are no guarantees it will ever pay off. You even risk losing money. That's part of starting a business and investing in it.

The good news is that you are your own boss. The bad news is that most business start-ups require total devotion on the part of their founders in order to have any chance of getting off the ground. If you were opening a restaurant, you would assume that anyone investing in your future would want to see proof that you're going to deliver. They would expect you to have a business plan and a budget. They would expect you to have a 1 year plan, a 5 year plan and a 10 year plan. They would expect you to have your initial investment money ready. They would hope that you use your time and talents wisely and associate with people who could help you expand your business. They would expect you to advertise and have a specific product you are selling with photos and commercials that illustrate your brand. They would expect the business to be more important to you than it is to the investors and for you to do most of the work. These would be bare minimum expectations from someone giving you money to invest in your start-up.

Just like any other business or product, you have to know what you're selling and whether it has value. A lot of people wonder if they are too much or not enough of something. It's true that most of the work goes to younger, better looking people or established names. That said, there's a little work for just about every type of person and there is a lot of work for more "average" people. You are probably not too tall or short, too thin or heavy, too ethnic or plain to get work, though you might find yourself limited in the kinds of work you are "right" for. Generally speaking, if you are over 30, you are too old to start a career as an actor. That said, I got my first movie at 31. John Mahoney was 42 when he started and 53 by the time *Frasier* came along. Harrison Ford, Gene Hackman, Rene Russo, Danny Glover, Tony Shalhoub, Whoopi Goldberg and Steve McQueen were all in their 30's when they began working. Danny Trejo was in his early 40's before launching a career that includes almost 180 movies and over 50 TV shows so far. Kathryn Joosten began her career at 46, moved to L.A. at 56, was cast as *The West Wing*'s "Mrs. Landingham" at 60 and started her Emmy-winning run at *Desperate Housewives* at 66. Charles S. Dutton was 34 when he got his start but he had bigger mountains to climb. Dutton was arrested at 17 for manslaughter. He served 3 years and another 3 years on a weapons charge. While in solitary confinement for 6 days, he was allowed one book and accidentally grabbed a collection of black playwrights. Afterward, he petitioned the warden to start a drama group. He earned a Master's degree from the Yale School of Drama and went on to win a Tony at 33 for the Broadway production of *Ma Rainey's Black Bottom* before starting his film and television career. These stories are the exception and not the rule but they prove that you can find work, no matter your look or circumstances.

It may be boring and no fun to handle your acting career like a business, but like the money you should save up to move to L.A. or pay SAG-AFTRA initiation fees, you probably won't regret it. It may be boring to think about health insurance, but I consider it in my goals every year just like any business owner would. Having your affairs in order gives you confidence. Setting goals gives you direction. You may never get that Oscar, but maybe you'll get to work with that director you always wanted to while trying. Setting goals helps you decide which things to say yes to and which things to turn down. Say yes to anything that takes you closer to your goals in any way.

Most people work at least 40 hours a week. Start-up business owners can easily work 90 hours a week for awhile. The good news is that, in the entertainment industry, there are a lot of things you can call "work." Time on the shooting range, learning to ride horseback or going to the gym can all be considered work. Going to a fashion show or eating lunch at an agency hangout can be work. If you're willing to see everything as an opportunity, work is all around you.

It's none of my business, but a word on what I've learned about money. First, a moment of praise for Lucille Ball and Desi Arnaz for inventing the rerun and, therefore, the residual. Whether you do a movie, TV show or a commercial, you should receive residuals– eventually. When actors work, we make a fair amount of money per day or per week. But we don't work most days or weeks. Even people who work a lot don't always work a lot. So it's good to keep in mind that, no matter how big the check, this too shall pass. Very few actors get to work a lifetime. Less than 1% make enough to live. Plan accordingly.

When I was starting out, like 95% of actors in the union, I made less than $5000 a year as an actor. It was very hard to get auditions and even harder to get parts and none of it was enough to keep paying my rent. It could get discouraging to see so little come from my efforts. I decided to tithe to myself. I'd pay my agent 10% of the gross (the total I earned), then buy myself a gift for 10% of the net (the money left after paying taxes and commissions). I was allowed to use the rest for electricity and food. I bought myself those gifts to keep my spirits up in the face of all that rejection, all those dashed dreams. As soon as I made over $10,000 in a year and could actually start to sorta live off my acting, I switched to tithing myself 1% of the net. My mother calls these treats, "hyacinths for the soul." All I know is they were tangible rewards for those lottery wins without affecting my net worth. That's sustainable. That's enjoying the fruits of your labor without spending like you'll always make this much money in a day. A day on a commercial can easily lead to $15,000. I found that not being seduced or confused by the excitement of the windfall let me live off of acting without waiting tables and that was worth not having a new car.

For me, freedom is the only thing money can buy that's worth having. I never owned the latest Prada bag, but I also never had to cover my shift waiting tables so I could go to an audition. My days are free to work on my career full time. By keeping my bills low and consistent, I have the freedom to audition and prepare which allows me to put my career first. Its none of my business how you pay your bills or when you buy a car, but if you want to live off of acting, this spending plan can offer freedom and time and that's always been worth a lot to me.

Setting Goals

Dare to dream big and set daunting goals for your future. Set goals for 5 - 10 years from now and let your imagination run wild.

Do you want to produce or direct? Buy your mom a house? Get a star on the Walk of Fame? Have a sandwich named after you? Travel the world? Own your own jet? Appear on the cover of *GQ*? What are your wildest fantasies for how far your career could take you?

Then it's time to get real. This is a business. After you set your lofty goals for your bright and beautiful future, think backward. If your 5 year goal is to win an Academy Award for best actor, then you will need to be in movies, preferably ones with Academy-friendly directors or cast members. You will need a starring role and you will need to be amazing. If you've already joined the union and gotten an agent and started building your resumé and reel, maybe you need to focus on meeting directors or on finding a coach with an Academy Award-winning track record. If you've achieved all these things, maybe it's time to sign with a more powerful agent or hire a publicist or produce a screenplay with the perfect role for yourself. For each stage of your journey, there are always many paths you can choose on your way to your goals. Just keep thinking forward.

Every January, I like to write down goals for the year. I brainstorm my 5 year goals and ask myself things like, "If I want to be the first female director on the cover of Vogue in 5 years, what can I do this year to get closer to that goal?" I'd need to direct a feature. I'd need to research and hire a publicist or befriend someone at Vogue. I'd do well to make some red carpet appearances wearing exciting designers.

Once I've listed my goals for the year, I break those down into what I call, "do-ables." These are goals you can cross off a list and consider them achieved, usually within a week or so. If the goal is too big to accomplish within a week, perhaps it needs to be broken down further. "Direct a feature" is too big a goal, even if you've already directed before. Borrow a camera, trade in a favor to cast a star, and shoot a "trailer" may put you closer to your goal. "Shoot a trailer" is a pretty big goal too and might be handled better as do-ables. Maybe your to-do list would include finding free crew, securing a location and creating a shot list.

Sometimes our goals fuel us, other times, they make success feel like a far away dream. Turn dreams into goals and goals into do-ables. It may not be as fun to think about the steps it takes to achieve a dream, but this is a business, not a dream.

When to Join SAG-AFTRA

If you're already a union member, feel free to skip this part. If you aren't a union member and wonder if you should become one, the answer is YES if you plan to work as a professional actor in film and television. Being part of the union is a basic tool in the same way a liquor license is a tool for a new bar. It is your license to operate as a professional. There are several ways to become eligible to join the union and you should check the website to find the latest rules and regulations. At the time of this writing, the site is http://www.sagaftra.org/home. It used to be a true "catch-22" to qualify to join the union. You had to be hired to work on a union job but union jobs would only hire union actors. Being hired for a union gig is still the strongest and best way to join the union, if only because you will receive union pay for the job. You'll need it to pay the initiation fee ($3000 at the time of this writing) and the first semiannual dues (currently $99).

The second, far easier way to become SAG-AFTRA eligible is to work for a minimum of 3 days as a background actor on a union project. For people living in Los Angeles, New York, Louisiana and other secondary markets, this should be a snap. But, then you're stuck footing that big initiation fee without an initial investment in your business. And the truth is that, on many sets, the background players can be treated pretty poorly in comparison to their principal counterparts. That said, joining the union will significantly increase your day rate so it will all even out if you keep working. If you look at this career like a business, think of it as sinking only your own money into a start-up company versus having a believer in the industry willing to bet on you.

That said, there's nothing wrong with using background work to enter the industry. Plenty of people have done it, though few will admit it. When you're starting out, it's good to be on sets and observe what the job really is, how it all works and just why it usually takes at least 200 people to make a movie. And you never know what could happen when you're on a movie set. Though it doesn't happen as often as you'd like, thousands of people have joined the union as a result of being given a line while working as a background player. It's like the lottery, "You gotta play to win." You certainly won't be given a line sitting at home judging background players.

The last way I know of that you can join the union is, under the new merger agreement, to have been affiliated with any other performance union for at least 1 year and have received work as a principal in that union. Whether you belong to ACTRA, AEA, AFTRA, AGMA, or AGVA, your dues to that union must be paid in full when you apply to join SAG-AFTRA.

There are advantages to staying non-union while you're trying to build your reel and resumé and some people like to wait to join the union long after they become eligible. I did. When you're starting out, you need to get experience and you need to accumulate "tape" on yourself. (For you young people, before YouTube or DVD's were invented, we used to put our acting reels on things called "tapes"). When you're doing background work, if you are featured in a project, you may be able to use that tape later for a montage opening (or closing) of your reel once you gather a scene or two with speaking parts. Though it may be very difficult to get even one line on a union movie or TV show, it can be far easier to land a sizable part on a student film or non-union project. Later in your career, it may require some negotiating to star in your next-door neighbor's non-union film, but when you're non-union, you're entitled to take a chance on your cousin or your friend from class.

By staying union-eligible but not joining the union, you can put "SAG-AFTRA Eligible" on your resumé and still take non-union jobs. Many people, including me, believe you can just put "SAG-AFTRA" as long as you know you can find the money for the initiation fees within 24 hours at any given moment. If you're serious about working in this industry, you must be prepared to pay those fees at any time or you are not ready to work. You never want to get caught lying on your resumé, but if you are union eligible and have made preparations to join the union at any given moment, it isn't a lie to say that you are a union hire.

The fees to join the union may seem like a lot of money to keep lying around, especially when you're broke. Then get a credit card and keep that balance available or arrange in advance to borrow the money from someone you can trust. If you planned ahead before making your move to L.A., you should already have this money in the bank. If not, work it out. No one cares about your special circumstances, they just want to know if you can deliver. If not, NEXT!

If you join the union by getting vouchers from background work, the money is mostly coming out of your pocket. If you just make yourself eligible and keep working, then when you land that commercial or your first guest star on a TV show, you'll have a bunch of money coming to you to help pay back your investment. I think that was the original intention. I don't think the union intended to make the initiation prohibitively expensive, just an initial investment in your career. Don't look at the money as a roadblock– look at it as buying stock in your own company knowing it could pay off like a software company going public one day.

If you're not SAG-AFTRA eligible and you don't want to do background work, commercials are an excellent way to get union work. Even some films will take a chance on a newcomer, but you'd really have to wow the Bigwigs. Most agents will not want to sign someone who isn't at least SAG-AFTRA eligible.

Photos

Your photo is often the first marketing tool people see. Take the time to check out different photographers and ask actors, agents and casting directors who they like. Many agencies have a a list. Set appointments to meet with the photographers and look at their books. Do you recognize anyone–a friend, classmate or celebrity? Do they look like themselves on a good day? There's an old saying in building–measure twice, cut once. Spend the energy to research before you shoot with someone and you can avoid wasting money on photos that don't work. Your cousin may be talented and free, but if they don't understand what a headshot needs to do for you, they are still a waste of time and money.

Make sure your photos are up to date and reflect the types of parts you find yourself booking. The best photos look like you on a good day. Your hair, eye and skin colors should be accurately represented. It's fine to edit out a wrinkle here and a dark shadow there, but it's important to represent your age range accurately. One of the most common complaints of casting directors and agents is that they called in an actor because they loved their photo only to find the person looks nothing like the photo. I wish I had a dollar for each time I've heard casting people complain, "I loved the photo, I would've hired that photo, but the person in that photo never showed up." No glamour or fitness shots unless that's the only career you're shooting for. It's okay to look a little sexy, glamourous, comedic or tough in your shot, but don't get too carried away portraying one type of character as it could limit your casting.

It's fine to have more than one shot, but they should be distinctly different. Typically, a commercial shot requires a smile or pleasant expression and a theatrical shot requires a little more intensity. You can also choose a shot that includes more of your body and another that features only your face. In general, commercial shots should include more of your body and accurately represent your size and shape. You may want to try a shot that shows the direction you'd like to take your career. A former child actor may want a shot that showcases their newfound maturity without alienating the people who liked their work. Someone who always plays "bad guys" may want to try a photo that focuses on their ability to play more nuanced characters. If your representation can handle two different photos, select one that will keep getting you the work you know you can book and use another for the direction you'd like to take your career.

Your photo should be recent, but there's no need to get new photos more than once a year unless your physical appearance changes. If you cut your hair dramatically or change the color, you should get headshots that reflect the change then update any websites and work-related social networking sites with the new photos. If your weight or age appearance changes dramatically, you should consider new photos. Otherwise, photos of adults can easily last 3 - 5 years. The younger you are, the faster your face changes so photos should be updated more frequently.

Choosing your photo is not a one-man job. Your photographer may indicate their favorite photos. If you have representation, give them the contact sheets or 4x6's or a link and they will vote on their favorites. Lastly, I like to hand the photos over to friends and colleagues for their votes. In the best case scenario, you will find some consistent winners, photos everyone likes. If you still have any question which one to pick, look at headshots of other people in your category. Would your photo stand out in a stack with theirs?

I like to prepare for the shoot by thinking ahead about wardrobe and posing. I've asked my agents for some of their favorite client photos and they've been happy to hand a few over. These are photos that are getting people work, so pay attention to what's effective for a headshot. Choose clothes and styling that reflect the characters you are most often called in for. If you usually play jovial dads, wear a simple Midwest-type (again, get over the offensiveness of it all and just go with it) shirt and a warm expression, maybe even a smile. You may want photos of yourself looking provocative, but if you normally get cast as a high school kid, save the push-up bras and low-cut shirts for when you look older.

I also go through magazines looking for shots that grab me and poses I may want to try. Sometimes I bring a few of the magazine pages or agency headshots with me to show the photographer. I choose shots that have the cropping I like or the tone I'm going for. A picture is worth a thousand words so bringing a few can keep communication brief and accurate. Some photographers may take it the wrong way if you show them someone else's work. To avoid this, I ask if they'd mind me showing them a photo or two to help me make myself clear. As long as you don't come across as telling them how to do their job, they should be happy for the help.

Unless you're damn sure you know what you're doing, women should hire a makeup artist. Many photographers will offer one but it's okay to use your own. As with the photographers, it is wise to check out the makeup artists book or website. Someone who specializes in stage makeup or fashion may not be the right choice even if you can get them for free. It will cost a lot more to shoot twice than to get it right the first time. Even if you get everything for free, it can still cost you. Your agents may not be happy and may even see you as "green," amateurish or not committed. Worse, your agent may send ineffective photos out and cost you months of your career waiting for a phone that won't ring.

Resumés

The first marketing tool people usually see is your photo. The next is your resumé. Some agencies have a specific layout they use. Some require that you use their logo. You can find many examples of actor's resumé templates online. Always put your most recent work first. Remember that this is a marketing tool. Double check the spelling of all names and titles. It's okay to handwrite a recent credit on a paper resumé, but, in this day of home printers and electronic resumés, try to keep your resumé as current as possible. As to when you can add to your resumé, you can add a new credit the moment you book the job. Some people prefer to wait until after they complete the job, just know that sometimes you book a job months in advance. You may also keep a credit on your resumé even if you're cut from the final project. The resumé is giving you credit for the work you've done, regardless of the outcome. As such, if you are released from a project before doing the work, you should not expect to take credit for the work. Some projects require that you sign a letter of confidentiality. If so, you may be restricted in what you can announce, but generally speaking, if you book a part, you're allowed to say you booked it and put it on your resumé.

Many people, when they are starting out, "pad" their resumé or just flat-out lie. When I was casting to shoot 8 minutes of my script *Lone Star Trixie* starring Richard Dreyfuss, there was someone who'd put my short film, *Intermission,* on their resumé. Though it was flattering, I knew for a fact they hadn't worked on the project and it made me mistrust them. L.A. is a small town and everyone talks. If you lie, you will probably get caught. Almost everyone does at some point. Focus on getting work and the resumé will take care of itself. If your acting school graduation play was in an off-Broadway theatre, it's fine to list it as a play in that theatre and not clarify that it was a graduation play. But if you've never done that play or been in that theatre, you will end up meeting someone who dated your costar or knows all the lines or something. If you only fudged a detail, the Bigwigs probably won't even mention it. If you lied, it will change their perception of you and eat at your credibility. Then, when you're telling the Bigwigs about all your great scenes in an upcoming movie or TV show, they're skipping ahead to when you tell them you were cut to cover your next fake credit. It used to be popular for ingenues to say they were the girl who kissed "Elliott" in *E.T.: The Extra-Terrestrial.* I guess they figured no one would know what she looked like grown up and no one would bother to check in a pre-internet world. Though many of them were caught, I'm sure one or two of them got work from it. It appears to be a victimless crime as it never stopped the real "Pretty Girl," Erika Eleniak, from working on *Baywatch*, *Under Siege* and dozens of other projects since the 1980's. For me personally, it's not worth the risk of losing your credibility just to add a credit or two, but it probably won't end your career so do what you're comfortable with.

Follow up with IMDb to make sure they updated you as well. IMDb is the International Movie Database, an online resource used by almost everyone in the industry. Most productions will get to updating IMDb sooner or later, but if your name doesn't appear or a correction is needed, updates can be made by anyone with IMDb Pro. IMDb Pro is used as a quick reference by almost everyone in casting and production. In addition to the information seen on IMDb, the site also contains information about upcoming projects and includes your weekly ranking, an assessment based on how much your page is looked up and how much web activity there is around your name. The lower your number the better, because number one is the best. Twitter, Facebook, website traffic and a project release can all lower your number but don't get too caught up in it as the best way to lower your number quickly is to die. Sad, but true. As of today, Nicole Kidman has five movies coming out in the next year or so and her number is 193. Marilyn Monroe hasn't done anything since 1962, but her number is 196. That said, people do notice if your number is very high, indicating that you are probably new, or if it is very low, indicating you have excitement around your name.

When we were casting *Hell Ride*, there were several times that I tried pitching actors who weren't well known. In each case, the director and the other producers would ask to see their IMDb page. If I couldn't find a photo online within less than 1 minute, the Bigwigs would usually move on. Make sure your IMDb page is updated and features at least one photo of you. You can also upload your actor's reel so everything is in one place the next time someone thinks of you at a casting session. At $15.95 a month or $124.95 a year, you may also want to consider investing in IMDb Pro. It's a tax write-off and a great way to find out what your favorite director is doing next.

Reels

Another important marketing tool is your "actor's reel," a compilation of clips from your career. The length of your reel should correlate with your level in the business and the quantity as well as the quality of tape you have on yourself. If you're still in the early stages of your career, 3-4 minutes should be more than enough time to show people your work. If you've been at this for awhile or you have had an exceptional career, people are willing to watch (or at least fast-forward) through 10 minutes of material. The best acting clips feature you as the focus of the scene and have some arc in them where we get to see you make strong choices well. That said, the best clips to actually get people to watch your reel are scenes that feature you with a TV or movie star.

Open strong, finish strong. Choose clips that feature you as the center of attention. Be ruthless in your assessment of the clips you include. Take an honest look at everything you have available and choose wisely. Remember that the person watching the reel may not know anything else about you. This may be your first impression with some people, so try to be objective about the impression the reel will leave. Newer material should be featured in the first few clips. Include both dramatic and comedic pieces on your reel if possible. It's best to label each clip with the title of the show so that viewers focus on your work rather than trying to guess the name of the movie or TV show. Some people like to open or close their reel with a montage of clips from several pieces. It's good to show off your range a bit, but if you just want to show your many different "looks," it may be better to put this in your montage. The best montage clips include TV or movie stars, action sequences (fight scenes, sports scenes), dramatic changes in your physical appearance (period pieces, monster make-up), facial expressions (a wink, laughing) or physical expressions (slamming a table, flinching when startled). For the body of the reel, choose your strongest acting scenes over ones that show another look you can achieve. Robert Downey, Jr. didn't get the part in *Tropic Thunder* by proving he could play a blue-eyed Australian who became surgically Black. He got the part because he's proven he can act.

The last question I ask myself when deciding what to include on my reel is, "What direction would I like my career to take next?" When I was starting out, I often played the part of the "perfect girlfriend" (who would lose the guy to the "quirky girl"). It was great but I wanted to play roles with more depth. After *Enemy of the State*, I had tape proving I could play "the girl you didn't know would 'go there,'" characters who appeared to be respectable, but had a hidden darker side. I went through my old tape and found clips that would highlight this idea so that viewers could imagine me in a variety of more complex roles.

Make an honest assessment of the quality of material you have then put your best and most recent stuff first. Don't bore people. If you have a line at the beginning of a 3 minute scene and another line at the end, have your editor help you cut the middle of the scene out. It's good to keep a story flow in each tape clip if possible, but it's more important to keep things short and sweet than to tell the story of the scene. It's better to have a really solid 2 minute reel than a padded 4 minute reel that inspires fast-forwarding.

Be sure to include contact information at the end of the reel so that anyone viewing it can find you through your representation. If you don't have representation, include a phone number or email address that you don't mind strangers having. Some people like to include a few seconds showcasing their headshot with the contact information. If your reel is on a DVD, be sure the actual DVD is properly labeled with your name, representation and contact information as well as the running time of the reel. As with photos, it's best to spend the time and money to find the right editor to do your reel. There have been a couple of times when I wasn't available for callbacks and have had to offer my reel instead. Presenting a reel I can be proud of that shows what I can do is almost like nailing an audition. I've twice booked jobs in this way which makes my reel a worthy investment.

Social Networking

With social networking, it's possible to post on sites like Facebook to let people know you've booked something. Many casting directors now have Facebook pages. If you see that they have thousands of "friends," it's possible that they would "friend" you. Some even use their site to notify people of unique types they are looking for or background work available. If the casting director "friends" you and is using their page in this way, it would probably be fine to announce your good fortune on their page. The post may even be seen by other casting directors they've "friended."

Get your marketing materials together first; your headshot, resumé, reel and, if you think you have enough marketing material to support it, a website. Call anyone who gave you a business card. This will be much easier to do if you've used those business cards to stay in touch once in awhile. Some actors have twitter accounts or blogs. If you don't, maybe you should. Social networking is open to everyone now and can be a very useful tool for connecting with work. Remember this is a business. Just as your outgoing phone message shouldn't embarrass you if Spielberg calls, your social networking should reflect a professional actor. I have two Facebook pages, one for business only and one that includes personal photos and ideas. Neither page includes anything that would embarrass me professionally. Actors live in the public eye. Don't EVER put your home address on any networking site. Don't help stalkers by listing daily routines and where to find you. Don't post photos of yourself downing a beer bong or making out with someone. Social networking is a marketing tool and should be treated as such.

Their are also websites that give actors direct access to casting, like Actor's Access and LA Talent. Many agents require that you register with one or more of these services but they are usually open to any actor with a headshot and resumé. The more ways you put yourself out there, the more likely you are to catch someone's eye.

Agents and Managers

Your representation is another marketing tool. In an ideal world, your agent will seek out parts you're "right" for, pitch you and fight for you. In reality, most agents submit your materials and field calls on your behalf. They negotiate contracts and make sure the terms are fulfilled. They act as liaisons between you and the work. You receive 90% of the money, expect to do 90% of the work. As with the photographer and editor, you should research agents and managers before you hire them to represent you. Who else do they represent? Do they have a good reputation? Are their people working? Most contracts last 1 - 3 years, so choose wisely.

If you're shopping for an agent or manager, the time to do it is when you have work. Maybe you thought you'd get the agent first, then the work, but agents are attracted to working actors, not projects and potential. Maybe you think it's better to sign with someone crappy than to have no representation and maybe you're right. I've always had a commercial agent and I know of no other way to be seen for commercials. That said, if you add up all the years I was signed with a theatrical agency in L.A., you could still count them on one hand. I did have a manager, Marilyn Black, for 10 years.

Marilyn was great at schmoozing and she rarely took "no" for an answer. After she retired, I had no theatrical representation for the next 10 years of my career. None. I was no longer able to figure out how to get guest starring roles on TV, but I kept working in film by producing my own work and pursuing my connections. I'll admit that I like having an agent, but even when I'm with a hardworking, well-respected agency, it's still on me to create my best career. No one cares more about your career than you. It falls upon you to be responsible for your career. If your agent isn't getting you work, find your own work and happily give them the 10% for handling all of the phone calls and contracts. Sure, keep your eyes open for a better agent but it puts the relationship into a better context if an agent seeks you out to represent you. When an agent comes looking for you, it shows initial investment and belief on the part of the agent so they're more likely to fight for your career and care if you succeed. Even so, many agents have short attention spans if you don't start making money right away.

In most secondary markets there are plenty of agents who don't use contracts and some markets even allow you to have more than one agent representing you theatrically or even commercially. However, in Los Angeles, there's usually paperwork and exclusivity involved. Some agencies may offer to "hip pocket" you, send you out without signing you. Though this may be a good way to try out an agency or get your foot in the door of a big agency, being hip pocketed also means you are likely not a priority unless you make them some money.

Speaking of money, never pay an agent up front. The business model for representation is that they make their income as a percentage of your earnings. If you're not making money, you shouldn't be paying them any money. This industry preys on people's dreams. There are unscrupulous "agencies" that say you have to pay them fees for any number of things. Some have cut deals with photographers to offer you a portfolio. Portfolios are for models only and should include photos and tear sheets from a variety of photographers, not a day in a studio with the same guy who shoots all their clients. Likewise, there are some "agencies" that say you must get your headshots from their photographer. This should be a red flag to you indicating that they may be interested in making their money off of your dreams and not your work.

You're Always Hottest When...

I'll admit up front that this is not my strongest area of expertise. I've spent a lot of time around celebrities and I figured out fairly quickly that it wasn't a life I wanted. I love acting and I'll admit that it can be fun to walk red carpets and attend award shows, but I remain unwilling to have people care what's in my trash. That said, I did spend a lot of time around celebrities. I've had my share of moments in the sun and I've noticed some things.

Unless the stars align for you, you're always hottest before the movie or TV show comes out. The hotness clock starts when you book the job. If the job is anticipated, like the next Spielberg movie or the newest series from David E. Kelley, that heat rubs off on you. Check your IMDb Pro numbers if you doubt me. Until the series airs or the movie is released, your part is every scene you shot and every line you said. When the public finally views it, you may have been cut out entirely. Before it comes out, the show is going to be a hit, the movie is going to receive nominations. Afterward, it may be the biggest flop in town.

As I've said, my first small part in a big movie was in the sequel to *Terms of Endearment*, one of the most beloved movies of the 80's. It had been more than a decade, but both Shirley MacLaine and Jack Nicholson were reprising their Academy Award winning roles. Award winners and nominees: Ben Johnson, Juliette Lewis and Miranda Richardson also starred. The large cast was a veritable who's who featuring Bill Paxton, Scott Wolf and Marion Ross. The director, Robert Harling, was also the writer. He'd written the hilarious *Soapdish* and the classic *Steel Magnolias*. Hopes were very high. Not only were all but one of my scenes and all but one of my words cut, the movie was considered a bomb. It opened in 10th place, grossing $3.3 million for the weekend. Up until the movie came out, I was starring as "Sitcom Actress Becky" in a hotly anticipated sequel to a beloved classic alongside some of our greatest actors. After, I was the girl in the "Good Witch Glinda" costume in a flop relatively few people saw.

The time before a project is seen by the public is an opportunity to be part of the excitement that surrounds it. If no ones heard of the movie, it's a chance to promote it. There are times when a movie or show comes out and it's a bigger hit than anyone anticipated. Nobodies became somebodies after *My Big Fat Greek Wedding*. That said, it is wise to remember the movie could be *The Big Chill*, but what if you are Kevin Costner on the cutting room floor? Then you will truly wish you'd done all you could to make the most of the time before the film was released. Costner's scenes were all short flashbacks and casket shots, but that's a heck of a lot more than not one frame of film. We rarely regret the things we do, but the things we don't do can dog us for a lifetime. Take a chance. Invest in yourself and help others see why they should invest in you.

If you do get cut, remember that you're in good company. Michelle Monaghan was cut from *Constantine* even though one of her scenes was the director's favorite scene in the movie. Uma Thurman was cast as Blake Lively's mother in Oliver Stone's *Savages* but failed to make it to the screen. Jon Stewart was cut from *First Wives Club*. Michael Biehn reprised his role in *Terminator 2: Judgement Day* only to have it disappear and Andy Garcia was excised from *Dangerous Minds*. Rachel Weisz, Michael Sheen, Jessica Chastain and Amanda Peet were all cut from Terrence Malick's *To the Wonder*. Mickey Rourke, Martin Sheen, Billy Bob Thornton, Gary Oldman, Bill Pullman, Lukas Haas and Viggo Mortensen were all cut from Malick's *Thin Red Line*.

You can't control the project, but you can control what you do with the time leading to the release. Prep all your marketing materials. Even the smallest part deserves some attention. You probably won't be able to add anything to your acting reel until after the public sees the project, but you can make sure your reel is up to date, professionally edited and available for viewing online. When you add the piece, make sure to let people know you updated your reel. Post a link on your social networking page, send postcards or emails to casting directors, directors and producers you've worked with, or agencies and managers you're targeting. Reach out to stylists and designers if you will be attending the premiere. After you've done what you can to be unforgettable in the film, use your momentum to bring you to the next level.

Hiring a Publicist

If you already have a career or if your part is fairly large, it may be time to hire a publicist–at least for the few months leading up to your project's release. In the interest of full disclosure, until now, I hadn't retained a publicist for more than a day, mostly because acting is my sole source of income and I don't live large. That said, they can be money very well spent. The publicists I have worked with on red carpets have been very helpful. They let you know who you're interviewing with and they prepare the upcoming photographers as you go down the line by telling them about your part. Not to mention my last name must often be spelled and they handle that. But the main reason to hire a publicist is because you are always hottest before your movie comes out.

As I said, before the movie comes out, the film is a winner and your part is all of your lines and scenes. As such, you may find that you can attend other people's premieres and be photographed on the red carpet. If the movie is a highly anticipated blockbuster type, you may find a publicist can get you on award show carpets. Some have the pull to get you featured in magazines, on late night shows and on radio shows. Smaller publications may even want you for a cover. You tend to get what you pay for. A publicist who charges $1500 a month may not have the kind of access that someone charging more than $3000 a month has. Publicists with less access can still get you on red carpets for gallery openings and fashion shows as well as nightclub and charity events. They should have connections to press and some publicists also know designers, stylists and jewelers to help with red carpet looks. As you would with an agent or manager, look at their client list to see if they're getting their people out there.

If you decide to retain a publicist for some time, it is fairly standard to commit to 3 months of working together to make the most of your moment. Most major magazines require 3 - 6 months lead time to include an article or photo shoot and television shows require advance notice to include you in their line-up. If you feel certain that the film will make a splash, it may also be a good idea to retain your publicist for at least a month after the project's release to make the most of your momentum.

Though I'm still very new to having a publicist on retainer, I have observed a few things. The process of retaining a publicist usually starts with a meeting where you lay out what's happening in your career and the direction you'd like to take it. It is wise to enter these meetings with a very clear idea of what you're selling. Think of yourself as a product. What would your slogan be? Who are you hoping to attract? How would you characterize this moment in your career? Where do you see your career going?

The publicist will then come up with a proposal within a week or so. The proposal will describe a press and marketing strategy as well as a price and time commitment. The first thing I look for is a meeting of the minds. If the proposal feels like the publicist didn't listen to you or wants to take you in a direction you're not comfortable with, that's probably not the right person for you. If the proposal makes you feel excited to get started, you may have found your winner.

Someone once said to me, "The way you do anything is the way you do everything." If the publicist is late for your first meeting or forgets to return your calls, that may be an indicator that you are not a priority or that they have poor follow up. If the proposal has spelling and punctuation errors, it may mean they have poor attention to detail. Pay attention to how they treat you before you sign because, just like on a first date, they are probably on their best behavior before they get the payoff. Your publicist is one of your closest team members so it is imperative that you trust them and have open communication from the start.

Once you choose your publicist, be prepared to do some work on your own behalf. It is very expensive to pay someone to wait around while you get your marketing materials ready so have all your ducks in a row before you begin meeting with people. You may want to bring a take-away for them; a list of your industry contacts and your connection to them, or a page of your reviews.

Once you begin working together, you will be expected to have a biography, a short description of you and your career. Be sure to gear your bio to showcase what you're selling, your "brand." As you prepare for interviews, you will be expected to be able to discuss the project, your part in the movie and the significance of your role. You should also prepare to speak about the director and your fellow actors. If you are working with much bigger names, interviewers will look to connect your name to those. Have short, fun stories ready or at least a compliment or two about each person you worked with directly. There's really no way to know what you might be asked during an interview but, in general, keep answers brief, avoid negativity of any kind and try to stay on topic. Do you have an upcoming project you are excited about? Ask your publicist what is the best and most organic way to bring it up within the interview. After all, you want to use this moment to discuss what is going on in your career but you don't want it to come across as selling something.

When it comes to red carpets, it's not a bad idea to have a list of designers you like in case your publicist is able to help you with red carpet looks. You may even want to keep a few photos of looks you are drawn to so you can start a dialogue about your style. In general, be ready to give your publicist every tool at your disposal to help them promote you. When you are asked for something, get it to them right away. You are paying for everyday that you procrastinate on a task.

If your part is smaller or the project release is limited, you may not want to invest in a publicist at this time. There are still things you can do to get press. Ask any studio and producer friends if you can attend their premieres then wear something noteworthy on the red carpet. If you haven't made friends in the industry yet, you can still call your hometown paper and news stations and offer to do an interview. It may not be national news, but it helps get the word out about you and your upcoming project.

Red Carpets

There are many occasions that call for a red carpet: premieres, award shows, openings, charity events and other random celebrity gatherings. For the purpose of this discussion, we'll use premieres. A red carpet is an opportunity. Sometimes the film will ask you to do the press line, sometimes you are even contractually obligated. Other times, you're not sure if they would want to photograph you. Maybe your career is going fairly well but it's not your movie. Generally speaking, if you have something exciting coming out, it may be worth the effort to impose yourself on the red carpet, even if you are just attending the movie. You will probably need a publicist or some other representative to make this happen if you don't have enough clout to do it on your own. That said, I once had my friend's cousin who had a degree in public relations walk me onto the red carpet of a movie I wasn't in.

If you are being photographed, you'll need to think about wardrobe. Consider the tone of the event. Is it Black Tie? Brown Tie, meaning work suits? Is it an edgier movie like a horror film? Watch award shows to see the differences between the elegance and grandeur of the Academy Awards versus the funky fashions at the MTV Awards.

I'm not going to tell you what to wear. What I will tell you is how to get clothes, assuming you don't have the cash to hire a stylist. If you are attending a premiere of a movie you are in, there's a good chance you can find someone who would like red carpet exposure. When I started walking carpets, my celebrity boyfriend paid for my dresses and, I admit, that made life a lot easier. But after our break-up and with only a couple of credits on my resumé, I had to fend for myself. There are plenty of reasons actors attend fashion shows, but one is in order to establish or further relationships with designers. If a model or make-up artist, or whoever, invites you to a runway show, go. The worst that can happen is you watch attractive young people walking in clothes for awhile.

I once went to a fashion show a friend was modeling in. He introduced me to the designer, Jerell Scott (who later went on to do *Project Runway* and *Project Runway All Stars*). I told Jerell I'd be attending the premiere for *Grindhouse* the next day. I was honest with him about not being in the film, but I was working on *Hell Ride* at the time and knew I had that to promote. It's always good to have something to promote, but it's really important if you're not in the movie you're attending. Jerell fitted the dress on me, I made a splash on the carpet and I returned the dress right after. I felt beautiful and regal. Jerell and I both got a LOT of exposure (pun intended if you've seen the dress) and it was free of charge for both of us.

Perhaps you know someone who owns a shop or someone trying to launch a line. If you don't know anyone in the fashion industry, it's time to pay more attention to what you like. In 2004, I watched the premiere of a new TV show–*Project Runway*. When I saw Austin Scarlett's amazing corn husk dress on the premiere episode, I was hooked. I knew I would have to wear one of his dresses. By the third week, I could take it no more. I started calling the production offices. I explained that I wanted to wear an Austin Scarlett dress on the red carpet. Then I got busy lining up a red carpet event to attend. I called the show's producers week after week, renewing my interest in wearing one of Austin's dresses. I lucked out and got invited to a small awards show so I called some more. A couple months of calls later, when Austin was finally cut from the show, my phone rang. Austin was happy to lend me a dress from the line he'd made for the finale–the dresses we never got to see because he was cut. He would be attending the screening of the show's finale in L.A. the same week as the award show, so he walked the carpet with me–his first red carpet.

Pay attention to what you like and reach out to the people who could provide you with it. I've been given footwear, fake hair, jackets, purses, gowns and more. You never know who else is trying to promote their brand. Sometimes a hair or make-up person may offer to do you for an event. If you're photographed, they can use those photos to promote their services. Look for symbiotic relationships. Create win-win situations. When I called *Project Runway*, I pointed out that they were a Weinstein Company production, that I'd already been in one of their movies and had another one coming out. Promoting me promoted them.

Remember that the red carpet is work. It's sorta like an office party, but not the Christmas party where you cut loose for one night with people you work with everyday who know you. This is more like a wedding of the boss' daughter. Yes, there may be dancing and drinking after the ceremony, but it's all on the boss' dime and under their watchful eye. The good news is that you have a good window of opportunity to get some time with your boss and network with other people. Have fun, be yourself, but have some respect for the occasion. Like a wedding, you are eating their food, drinking their beverages under a roof they provided with entertainment they provided. A premiere isn't about dresses, dancing and drinking any more than a wedding is at the end of the day. It's about the movie. The people in the bathroom line spent time and effort on this project. Anything negative you have to say about the movie or the event can and will be held against you. Treat the event like an opportunity to strengthen relationships and start new ones in a more personal environment while looking your best.

If you are allowed to bring a a guest, a "plus one," choose wisely. You may want to invite your manager or agent but you cannot expect them to act as your publicist on the red carpet. They may have their own agenda in attending the event and may even be disappointed if your part is smaller or less memorable than they'd hoped. Trust me, it can make for a crappy time at the after-party. Maybe you'd like to bring a date or a family member. If you're not well known, let your guest know that they will probably not be walking the carpet with you and that it is considered bad form to ask for autographs or photos. You will be judged by the company you keep. Urge your guests not to drink to excess. You never want to be the one who was asked to leave for bad behavior and your guest's behavior will be considered your behavior. I was once at a premiere after-party at a director's house. A TV star, who barely knew the host, brought an obnoxious friend who became more unruly as the night wore on. I watched as the host explained to the TV star that he needed to leave and take his friend with him. The host said he liked the TV star but that his friend was no longer welcome. Sadly, since the host didn't know the TV star well, the most memorable thing he learned about him was that he had bad taste in friends. I've never seen the TV star anywhere near that director again.

Premieres are parties but they are work parties. Consider yourself "on duty." Turn off your cell phone, bring someone you trust and take advantage of the opportunity to network. It's fun to meet actors, but focus on the people with the power to get you hired: producers, directors and studio executives. Listen more than you talk. Have fun and don't overindulge.

Waiting

There are moments in every career where it seems nothing is happening. Sometimes even when you have your marketing tools ready, you prepare for every audition and you're doing what you can to create your own momentum, nothing happens. At these times, your ability to wait will be tested. There are moments in every career where it will look like everything is coming together. Maybe you have a great and encouraging agent, your acting coach weeps at your genius and it's between you and Joseph Gordon-Levitt for the fourth lead in the next Scorsese movie. Then nothing happens. You don't get the part and your agent cools on sending you out. Waiting at these times can be excruciating. There are even moments in some careers where you just won an Oscar and nothing happens. I can only imagine that waiting of that sort can be hell.

Waiting frustrates. It feels like time is being wasted, like nothing is happening. The truth is waiting is an activity and done well, it can be time well spent. If your marketing materials need work, work on them. If you want to beef up your special skills, waiting can become preparing. You can use that time at the gun range or learning martial arts or training accents. Waiting can also be time used networking. Inventor Thomas Edison said, "Success is 10% inspiration and 90% perspiration."

The strange thing I've learned about waiting is that you never know what's really happening. I have invested a lot in striving to create opportunities for myself through writing, producing and directing. I have networked well and have created a reputation for being able to deliver on set. As a result of all that investing, occasionally, I have gotten an unexpected return on my investment. As David Carradine said, you never know which young filmmaker is watching you. Likewise, you never know when someone is pitching you or writing a part for you. What you can know is that you have to invest in yourself and in being unforgettable before you can expect the unexpected. Above all, the alternative to waiting is quitting.

The essence of waiting is an attitude, a reaction to things not going your way on your schedule. When I was waiting for *Django Unchained* to begin, I used much of the time working on my part, researching and finding inspiration. What I did not mention is that I was considered for three other movies during that time. If your career goes well, you will have to turn down a lot of work over time. Each time I got a call about another film, I reminded myself that I'd rather be on the *Django* set wishing I could've done those other movies than on their sets wishing I was doing *Django*. Rather than focusing on what I wasn't doing, I focused on the task at hand— creating unforgettable moments for Lara Lee.

During times when it all seemed to come together then "nothing" happened, I tried to remember that I couldn't know who I might have impacted. I reminded myself of times people thought of me and I didn't know about it. There was the time the casting director for *Friends* called me in off of a photo she had on file and many times people wrote parts for me. I reminded myself that I had many irons in the fire and that any of them might lead to work. Then I would double-down and try to add more irons and create more work for myself.

When there's no work in sight and it feels like it's been forever since you worked, it's hard to see waiting as potentially productive and good for you. I try to remember careers that have had big gaps in them. If you do this job your whole life, there may be gaps that span years. When I'm waiting for months for the phone to ring, I try to keep a long view and think how little time 6 months is in a 20 year career. I try to remember "The Lesson of the 100 Auditions," that I'd be fine being out of work for 5 months if I knew for sure that I was working in the sixth. Life as an actor requires more faith and better planning than most. Keeping money in the bank and room on a credit card is essential for a working actor. Working actors know that work comes and goes, no matter how famous or heavily lauded you are. It's hard enough to stay in good spirits while waiting without also having to panic about money.

When I was worn out with waiting and felt like I kept getting stuck in the same spot, my mother gave me a great image. She said life is too steep a climb to go straight up. It's more like a mountain with a road circling to the top. Each time you come to the northeast corner, you feel like you've already been there a thousand times but each time, the view is from a slightly higher vantage. Waiting may feel terrible and eat at your confidence and finances, but it is definitely part of an acting career. Even when you're working, a lot of your time will be spent waiting. Get good at it or suffer through it because the alternative is quitting.

Chapter 8:

Who You Know

Jeff Fahey once said to me when I was serving him a drink, "The only reason you're standing there and I'm sitting here is luck." I have no idea what kind of day he was having that inspired that comment, nor whether he's right, but I took notice. I'm not sure how much I believe in luck but I do know you can create your own opportunities for "lucky" things to happen.

We've all heard the saying, "It's all who you know." As someone who has worked with people who were friends first, I can say there's a lot of truth to that. And I worked with some of the same producers and directors again once they knew me and my work. That's part of the reason for the old saying, "Work begets work." The other part is momentum. Physics teaches us that a body in motion tends to stay in motion. Whether its because your name starts coming up more in casting conversations, because of the confidence working installs in an auditioner or because every job introduces you to more people in a position to hire you, work does tend to beget work.

So, one way to know people is to work. Ah, but that's a catch-22, a conundrum. Most actors think the person they most need to know to get work is a "good agent." If they have an agent and they aren't getting calls, they assume their agent sucks or that the agent is leaving them out of great auditions they see their friends attending. Maybe your agent does suck, but they only get 10% of the money. Should they really be expected to do more than 10% of the work? No one is going to care more about your career than you do. You may fulfill your dream of getting a "good agent" or of making some dissatisfied parent proud of you, but none of them can know what it means to sit in a room full of versions of you, waiting to be judged. In real life, as opposed to reality TV, your family is not usually in the waiting room after your first callback. I've been on hundreds and hundreds and hundreds of auditions and my family has only been to a couple auditions with me when their visits and vacations were interrupted by my unpredictable actor's life schedule.

Even the very best, most loyally devoted agent cannot possibly care more about your career than you do when you're working out to stay in shape in case you have to take your shirt off or learning to ride a horse for a western that loses its funding. During your highest highs and lowest lows, there will be very few people who understand what your life feels like, especially if it looks pretty great from afar.

Who you know comes in very handy if you don't have an agent. Many people have found success attending casting workshops where you pay a reasonable fee for the opportunity to audition for people (sometimes assistants, so be sure to ask) from various casting directors' offices. Some actors have been seen while doing plays, scene nights with a theatre company or in a well-connected class. I tried some of those things with some success, but after I'd trained for several years, I focused on getting on film. I did a film in New York that paid in subway tokens and meals. I did a day of background work on a Spike Lee movie so I could see how a great director works and what it was like to be on a big movie set. I did commercials so I could pay my rent and gather more snippets of tape on myself. Then I got industrious. I started creating work for myself. I met a producer during my summer serving drinks and we became friends. I'd met Richard Dreyfuss when I waited to speak to him after a play he'd done on Broadway. The producer was putting together a series of short films directed by movie stars so I put the two of them together and got a line as a waitress in the film. I now realize I probably should have also received an associate producer's credit, but live and learn.

Then I met someone in a bar. I was waiting for a friend when a man started chatting me up, trying to impress me with his knowledge of the National Security Agency (NSA). We exchanged factoids for a few minutes then I asked why he knew all these things. He said he was writing a screenplay about it. He asked why I knew so much, so I revealed that, at that time, my father was the number two guy there. The next thing I knew, he was setting up a lunch for me to meet the producers he was working with.

Maybe your father sells cars or runs a farm, but trust me when I say that you are far more likely to meet someone who's writing a screenplay about selling cars or life on a farm than about the NSA, especially when no one had heard of it. Whether you believe in fate, the law of attraction or coincidence, when you meet someone you never know who you're talking to or what they might find interesting. You are enough.

That same man, David Marconi, introduced me to a manager, Marilyn Black. She and I worked together for 10 years until her retirement and we remain friends today. Then Marconi took me to audit a class. The teacher was Ivana Chubbuck and, after years of working with her, she helped shape the actor I am today. Then David set up a meeting with the director of his script's film, Tony Scott. As you may have guessed, the film was *Enemy of the State*. Scott was very interested in my childhood, in what it was like to grow up the daughter of a spy. After about an hour of talking he said in his Australian accent, "You know, you're not what I thought you'd be."

"What did you think I'd be?"

"I thought your father was a geek and you'd be the daughter of a geek."

I smiled. "What do you think now?"

"Now I think you might be Christa."

After working with a coach, 3 auditions and several months, the part was mine. Yes, it was who I knew that got me that part. I knew my dad which helped me get to know David Marconi who introduced me to Marilyn Black, who would handle all of my auditions and contracts for the movie, and Ivana Chubbuck who coached me for the part. Then David connected me to Tony Scott who sent me to the casting director, Victoria Thomas. That led to the callbacks for Tony Scott and Jerry Bruckheimer. While shooting the film, I did some second unit scenes with one of the producers acting as director. Though another actor on set grumbled about working with a director other than Tony, I saw an opportunity to work with a producer who had an interest in directing, James W. Skotchdopole. That was in 1997. In 2011, I attended a dinner of producers for an upcoming Tarantino movie, one of whom was Jim Skotchdopole. The film's casting director? Vicki Thomas. The movie? *Django Unchained.*

At the end of the day, even knowing all those people, if I hadn't been good at what I do, I wouldn't have been given the part in *Enemy of the State.* I had studied acting in a conservatory for years, performed in off-off Broadway plays, auditioned for well over a hundred commercials and worked in TV and film by that time. I took scene study classes, worked with a private coach, practiced until I knew I had an original take on the material and several other options ready and then did a great job at three increasingly more intimidating auditions. Though I may have been given the opportunity because of who I knew, I wouldn't have gotten the part if I wasn't totally prepared. And that was just for a few scenes.

Film is a serious business with serious cash involved. People don't like to take chances. I decided that it was my job to give the Bigwigs no reason to not hire me. I was determined to make it easy for them to say yes to the well-connected girl. It is inevitable that if you live in L.A. long enough, you will come into contact with people in a position to hire you. It is up to you what you do with those moments.

The Company You Keep

If you stick around long enough, you run into the same people over and over, the ones with staying power. That's one reason why I found it important to associate with people who I could learn from, rather than people who wanted to sit at coffee shops talking about how much their agents sucked. I knew that what I'd learn at those afternoon coffee tables was how to struggle, how to blame others and how to talk about my goals instead of making them happen. There's a wonderful refrain in a song from *The Rocky Horror Picture Show*, "Don't dream it, be it." Dare to walk up to a Bigwig and use the opportunity well. Dare to talk to a stranger and be open to who they might be. Seek out people with more experience than you. Anyone who has staying power in this industry has something to teach you. Most people you start out with may be misguided, misinformed and inexperienced. Most will fade away, so it's good to form relationships with people who've been where you are and figured out how to stay relevant. Not only can they expose you to information, people and ideas, the odds are also better that they'll still be your friend and living in L.A. in 10 years.

Over the years, I've found that many people are willing to share their wisdom. Ask people about what they've learned, what they would do differently if they had it all to do again. Ask people how they achieved their success. When I was preparing to direct my first short film, I knew I had a lot to learn. First, I called all the actors I knew who had directed. Then I called all my director friends and asked them questions. At some point, I realized I'd only spoken to men so I thought about which female director I'd most like to learn from. I decided to target Betty Thomas, the highest grossing female director at the time. I asked my friends if any of them might have a connection to Thomas. These are the moments when it's good to have well-connected friends, whether they are masseuses, lawyers, assistants or industry insiders. I acquired her personal cell number then wrote a few notes for myself in case I got nervous and scattered. It was awkward at first with me rattling credits and dropping names while explaining the reason for the call. I explained that I'd gotten great advice but wondered if there was any wisdom specific to being a female director. In the end, she spoke to me for about half an hour and was very encouraging.

It's good to learn from people who have what you want or have achieved your goals. They may not all be receptive to you, but, if you're an actor, you can live with rejection. It's also important to seek out people who want what you want. I don't mean people who share your acting goals so much as people who value what you value. If you value having a family, then you might not want to choose too many friends who value cruising bars and shiny cars over things like saving for a house and having children. If you value privacy, you may not want to surround yourself with people who seek publicity. And vice versa. Figure out what you care about and try to keep company with people who care about the same things. That said, I've had many friends with values that didn't line up with mine but they truly valued me and that was plenty.

I have many different types of friends. Other than having gone to high school with *Entertainment Tonight*'s Kevin Frazier, my oldest friends are mostly not in the industry. During my training years in New York, I started to gravitate to my classmates who showed the most promise. I've lost touch with all but one of those people, Jernard Burks–the one who is still working. The others faded away as they left the industry and had less in common with me. While we were still in New York, Jernard got me in the habit of approaching actors after Broadway shows and asking them questions that might help me in my journey and create opportunities to connect in some real way. That's how I met Richard Dreyfuss, with whom I'm still friends to this day. Having someone like Richard in my life gave me the confidence and access to keep befriending people further ahead of me in this career. Filling my life with people who have more experience and success than I has given me more than just mentors, though that would've been plenty, it's given me the confidence to believe in my own talents and ability to have a career. Best yet, most of my industry friends are still in the industry. You won't know how important that is until the uncomfortable day that you get a lead in a movie while your friend waits on your table. They will want to be happy for you, but it's hard. It's pretty easy for me to be happy for a friend who wins another Oscar. I'm used to them being more celebrated than I am and I'm used to celebrating them myself. It's a little tougher when someone you started out with gets the cover of *Rolling Stone* while you wait for your agent to call. It may not be fair, but it's true. That said, I'd rather have to find it in myself to be happy for the other best actor from my old acting class than to have friends who have trouble being happy for me.

Protect your credibility. If you say you're going to do something, do it. If you say you're "friends" with someone, you ought to have their phone number and they should at least recognize your name. You never know who knows whom. Lying to make yourself look better almost always backfires. Not only are you likely to get caught eventually, you can end up being a joke. Be careful who you vouch for. If you recommend a friend and that friend disappoints or offends, it can stick to you. A friend of mine introduced our friends to someone who ended up swindling them out of millions. Though my friend did nothing wrong, he ended up leaving L.A. under a cloud. You will be judged by the company you keep but the bottom line is, this is a tough business and it's important to have friends you can count on.

I try to live by a few simple rules. One is never let someone sit in your bleachers and yell, "Yay other team!" As a Louisianian by way of Maryland, I know an interesting factoid about crabs. Did you know that you don't have to put a lid on a bushel of live crabs? If any of the crabs try to crawl out, the other crabs will pull them back in. I call this "the crab trap" and will do just about anything to avoid it. It may be tempting to find company in misery, but no good can come from surrounding yourself with people who drag you down with complaining and negativity. This business is tough enough without added drama. As much as possible, I try to keep my life a drama-free zone and save my energy for drama in front of the camera.

Co-workers and Colleagues

At work, your main focus should be doing a great job. Many celebrities eat in their trailers, wait between takes in their trailers, have their own hair and makeup trailers and generally avoid contact with everyone but the director and producers. Much of the time, their work speaks for itself and so should yours. That said, they've already made connections and work can be a great opportunity to network. Like the stars, you should concentrate on connecting with the producers, studio executives and the director. Do consistently great work and listen more than you talk and you should win most of the Bigwigs over. Additionally, you may meet A.D.'s, P.A.'s or fellow actors who may be involved in other projects or have connections you'd like to have. You never know who you're talking to, so listen more than you talk and you may get surprised. On one movie, one of the office P.A.'s co-owned a business with our director. Some people on set may be related to the higher ups. Your wardrobe person might be the personal dresser for your favorite actor. A background player might be a director trying to understand the job of an actor. You really just never know.

Networking is different than using people, mostly in intent. When I was getting my degrees in English Literature and Creative Writing, I hung out with other students and writers and spent time after class with teachers. I surrounded myself with people who were interested in the same things I was interested in. (Yes, two degrees in English and I still finish sentences with prepositions. Call me a rebel.) Gearing up to start my doctorate (which I abandoned to start my acting career), I was able to approach one of my old teachers about being my guide on that journey and my sponsor in the department. When I had all those after-class conversations with him during my undergrad years, it never occurred to me that I was laying groundwork for some future use. My intentions were confined to the present, not a stepping stone to some favor to be named later. When I met David Marconi, it never occurred to me that he could one day introduce me to my acting coach, my manager and Tony Scott. I was too busy having a compelling conversation with a knowledgeable and interesting stranger to think how it might all benefit me one day. When I met Quentin, of course I hoped to work with him some day, but I never mentioned that I was an actor. I stayed in the present, asked questions, listened more than I talked and enjoyed meeting someone fascinating. After over 3 hours of talking, it was another actor who recognized me and told Quentin he was a huge fan of me in *Enemy of the State* and *For Love of the Game*. It was the best possible way for Quentin to find out what I do for a living. Throughout the 20 years I've known Michael Jai White, I've pitched him for many projects because I believe in him as an actor and thought he deserved the work. When he directed his first feature, he returned the favor and I was cast in *Never Back Down 2: The Beatdown*. I never pitched him for movies hoping one day he'd direct a feature and repay the favor, I pitched him because I thought he was too talented to ignore.

I've been told that I'm great at "working a room." The truth is I just really like people. I find them fascinating. I enjoy watching them reveal themselves. I'm chatty and I like telling people stories. I'm always mindful that I don't know who I'm talking to. I've hung out with royalty, Kunta Kinte's granddaughter and the guy who invented Windows, all without knowing who they were when I met them. I was enjoying their company too much to bother to ask what they did for money. Be genuinely interested in learning more about someone, and you will be interesting. If you find yourselves being potentially useful to each other's careers one day–great.

Working on a project together can be a very bonding experience, but it is often like summer camp. There are private jokes and matching t-shirts and everyone promises to stay in touch then most don't. Be one of those people who makes an effort to follow up. If you do great work and have a good attitude on set, people are more likely to be receptive to any reaching out you may do in the future.

If you're just starting out, you may not be working yet. Take classes and join theatre companies. Do enough research to find good ones. Not only will you get better and more experienced as an actor, you will meet people who care about what you care about and are interested in what you're interested in. You may find yourself getting cast in someone's short film or even creating a project together. Sometimes casting directors need readers to run the lines off-camera during auditions. I worked as a reader for 3 days of commercial casting. Not only was I paid for my time, it also gave me several days to show the clients why they should hire me for the spot–which they did.

If you're truly serious about this career, the key is to find ways to stick around. Work begets work and many jobs are the result of who you know. You never know who you're talking to and you never know who anyone may become. Think ahead. You never want to start an audition owing someone in the room an apology. Most of the people I started out with have left the industry, but some of them went on to become directors, producers, celebrities, big-time agents, studio executives and writers for hit shows.

Sundance and Film Festivals

One of the best places to meet filmmakers is at a film festival. There are many festivals you can benefit from attending, but the Mac-Daddy of them all is Sundance. A common misconception is that you should wait until you have a movie there. My first trip to Sundance was because I had a movie in Slamdance, a smaller festival held at the same time in the same tiny town. I attended Sundance as often as possible and in every way possible. I went to movies, dinners, parties, after-parties and after-after-parties. I also attended films at Slamdance and some of the other smaller niche festivals held at the same time in the same tiny town.

I figured out many things but the most important was that I was foolish to let my pride tell me that I shouldn't attend Sundance until I had a movie there. It is more than enough to be a movie lover. Film festivals are for people who want to see movies before anyone else does with an audience of film lovers and who want to have an opportunity to speak with the filmmakers and stars. My hometown church group goes every year because the ski slopes are absolutely empty and they like to attend the Q&A sessions to learn more about the director's thoughts, ideas and experiences. If the senior set from my old church thinks they can go to Sundance without a movie opening there, certainly I can get over my silly attachments to the way I wanted to look in front of people. Most people at any festival understand that none of it happens without an audience of people willing to watch movies they know nothing about. There is no Q&A without an audience.

Sundance is very focused on directors. It's a great place to meet filmmakers who are starting out as well as seasoned veterans. To meet a lot of directors at once, try some of the short programs. Most short programs have between five and seven short films, which means there are usually at least five filmmakers there who got into Sundance. Make an effort to meet them or at least ask a thought-provoking question. If you do get to ask the director a question, be sure to follow up by introducing yourself afterward.

The bigger Sundance gets, the less access there is to everything. Restaurants have lines, movies sell out long before the festival begins and long lines wait at the will-call at 5 am. Parties are harder to get into and some movies even have a red carpet now. BUT, the best thing about Sundance from a networking standpoint is that it's the best place to meet a lot of people from every level of the industry very quickly and on more equal ground. In many ways, though they've incorporated velvet ropes and red carpets now, Sundance is a great democratizer. People don't have their cars. No one knows if you drive a Maserati or a Toyota. And people are bundled up so all those shapely bodies look a lot like the Michelin Man. There's no time for sleep, it can be crazy cold and, let's face it, most people in L.A. don't invest much in winter wardrobes so it's not the fashion show L.A. can be. In other words, moguls, models, actors and agents all have to let go of a little of their vanity and ego. It's a good thing, trust me, especially if you drive a Toyota.

Another big lesson was to bring a lot of business cards and a pen. Try to resist just getting people's numbers phone-to-phone and always give your card in either case. I find that, for actors, the best card has a photo of you, your cell number and your website if you have one. You may include the name and number of your representation but, for the purposes of Sundance, much of the card exchanging is about getting together for a party or Sundance event and they don't need your agent to be involved. I had a card especially for Sundance so that I could keep it simple. The first year I went, I had just slips of paper with my name and cell. People actually thought they were cute. By my fifth Sundance, my card had my photo, name, cell number and website. Still simple, but the photo helps jog their memory and the website gives them a place to find my reel and resumé.

Which brings me to the other thing I learned about business cards and the reason you need a pen. If you're meeting a lot of people, which you will, you may think that you'll remember them all. Some of you are reading this and are certain you would remember if you met the director of a short film who said they'd seen you in a commercial. But, what I found was that I met a LOT of memorable people at Sundance. Too many to remember. And whoa befall those less memorable–they were lost in a blur of sweaters and popcorn. Every single time someone gives you a card, take a minute to turn it over and write on the back. Write a physical description, like "fur hat" or "curly blonde." Then make a note about something that you talked about, especially anything you committed to. If you end up in a conversation in which you commit to sending someone a DVD of your last film or something, for goodness sake, do it!

Within a week or so after the festival's end, contact each person that gave you a card. Use the notes you wrote as a conversation starter. I usually feel an email is less invasive, but if someone told you to call, then call. Remember, you have something in common with anyone who ever gives you a business card–you were both in the same place for the same time for some reason.

The longer you wait to make the first contact, the harder it will be. Go 6 months without calling "fur hat" and you might not remember anything at all about the encounter. Also, we tend to feel less entitled to call the longer we wait. We fear they will have forgotten us. If you make the first contact right away, then it's totally appropriate to email them again when you get a part 6 months later, even if they never wrote you back. Emailing someone every 6 months is not "bothering" them, which is a common fear that sets in over time.

Sundance can be an amazing experience. I got to be there for the rare 4 minute standing ovation for *The Station Agent*. I made friends I still have today. The first year I went, I met the producer and two stars of the short film I didn't yet know I would later make. I got to throw snowballs, dance till dawn and relax in a jacuzzi.

There are often houses looking for someone to fill a bed. You may have to share a room and bathroom, but it's just where you sleep and you won't be doing much of that. Take a chance on Sundance and certainly attend any film festival in your area.

Talking to Celebrities and Bigwigs

Once you've found yourself in the same place at the same time with a celebrity, studio executive, director or some other bigwig, here are some basic conversation recommendations. Being interested makes you interesting. Most people like to talk about themselves. Put yourself in their shoes for a moment. Would it interest you to know you met some stranger in an elevator several years ago and they asked you for an autograph? Probably not. But it might interest you to know that someone read something you published or saw you play guitar in a coffee shop, especially if you're known for your acting. Try to put yourself in the other person's shoes. If you were an agent, would you care that your waiter was looking for one? Probably not, but it may interest you to know that your waiter saw you win a golf game. If you were a director, would it interest you to know that the girl behind you in line is looking for work? Probably not, but it may interest you that they saw the short film you did years ago. Though some actors and directors truly enjoy talking about their work with fans, put yourself in those shoes again. Wouldn't it be more fun, after all the interviews, press junkets and autograph signings, to talk about yourself rather than your work?

There were many times that I met producers, writers, directors, agents, managers and casting directors and had no idea who they were. Often, I didn't ask. I went to screenings, premieres and lunches at industry favorite restaurants and stayed alert and open. When I would meet someone I didn't know, I'd talk about where they were from, if they had children or how they knew the host. I try to ask questions that give the person an opportunity to reveal something about themselves. When I met Quentin, at some point I asked him what was the best thing that happened to him that day. He said that he was so glad I'd asked because he'd just figured out the ending to his script that day. He'd been puzzling it out forever and finally had an ending he was happy with. My question gave him a chance to celebrate his win with someone. For me, it revealed that he was open, optimistic and that he derived great pleasure and deep satisfaction from his work. I've known him over a decade now and I can say that it's all true.

The first and biggest thing to remember when you're talking to someone you look up to or someone who has achieved more than you have, is that they are people. They may not be "just like you," and many of them never went through whatever you're going through, but they are people just the same. Some people are shy and find talking to strangers hard. Some people enjoy meeting fans and having conversations with strangers, but not in the middle of a meal, during a break-up, while they're working or when they're in the bathroom. Yes, I know of more than one man who's been asked to shake hands at the most inopportune of moments.

People are bound to disappoint you at times. If your cashier at Wendy's lets you down, you probably won't remember it for long. If Harrison Ford or Eva Mendes disappoints you, you'll probably remember it forever. Maybe you'll even tell people that person is a "dick" or a "bitch" based on that one dashed expectation. Maybe you've wanted to meet Oprah Winfrey your whole life. You want to tell her how much she's influenced you and how great she was in *The Color Purple* and how she recommended what became your favorite book. Finally, the moment arrives. You spot Oprah on the street or at a shop or, best yet, on your set as your costar. Try to remember what it's like working as an actor. Some people are nervous, some like to run lines in their head, some people need to sit, focus and just breath. Now imagine that just before you have to be unforgettable on film, someone you never met before spends your last 5 minutes of prep time telling you how much you mean to them. Now imagine that you hear that speech from as many strangers as Oprah does. I'm guessing that both you and Oprah have moments where that speech might make your day and moments where it would feel inappropriate, frustrating or even frightening. Everyone is a person. Live by the Golden Rule as much as possible and do unto others as you would have them do unto you. If you spot Oprah shopping, take your shot if you must, but open politely. "Do you have a minute" or "Is this a good time for a compliment?" or at least, "Excuse me" or "I'm sorry to interrupt but…" You will find it easier to come in for a landing if you consider your approach.

If you only have one guaranteed moment with someone, I can't tell you not to take your shot. Many of my relationships in the industry have come from the moments I dared to introduce myself to someone I admired. I am saying to use your moment wisely. Be aware that you are asking them to pay attention to a total stranger at a moment that is convenient for you. This may be hard to understand, but when you want to tell someone you're a fan of theirs, you are actually asking for something from them. Many people ask for photos or autographs and all fans are asking for time and attention. Most fans are also expecting a positive experience so they are asking you to be up for the moment. Telling someone how great they are is actually not the same thing as having a conversation with someone. Listing reasons someone is great leaves them with very limited responses. Most people will say the same thing you would say, "Thank you." Not much of a conversation. Maybe you're different, maybe you want to take their time and expect a positive experience because you want to thank them. That limits their response to, "You're welcome." Again, not much of an exchange and probably forgettable. Remember that many people love their work and many people have stopped and taken their shot at telling those people about it when they found their chance. Remember to choose your moment wisely. Try not to approach anyone who's working with you until you're sure they have a moment to pay attention to you.

When you talk about you, don't talk about your career, especially not your sucky agent, especially if you're talking to another agent. They will see the future and see you complaining about them to some future agent. And, as always, you never know who you're talking to. They could be the owner of your agency or the wife of your soon-to-be ex-agent. If you're an actor, chances are you're good at other things too; sports, hobbies or crafts. Trust me when I say that most people would rather talk about knitting than your career. Some day-jobs are interesting. People who have children might enjoy knowing you work at a preschool. Pet lovers may like hearing about your dog-walking job. Sometimes you have something in common when you meet someone. Maybe you're at a wedding and you're both sitting on the groom's side. Maybe you've both chosen the same museum exhibit or off-off Broadway play. Those types of meetings allow you plenty to talk about without bringing up acting for awhile. "How do you know the groom?" "Have you been to this church before?" "Do you think the D.J. will play Kool & the Gang's *Celebration*?" "Are you a fan of this artist?" "Is this your first visit to this museum?" "Did you see the last exhibit that was here?" "Do you know someone in this play?" "Do you know this play?" "Have you been to this theatre before?" You don't have to be smart or well-informed to ask someone if they've ever seen anything else by this writer, if they know which exhibit is coming next or if they know how the bride and groom met. You just have to be interested.

On the topic of sucky, avoid all negative topics, and for goodness sake, don't introduce any. If you get stuck in a discussion about how some director's work is derivative or some actress should get her boobs done or how movies cost too much, remember that you don't have to add to the topic if you don't want to. If you feel you must speak your mind, remember that you never know who you're talking to so have your facts straight and be ready to agree to disagree.

When someone truly enjoys the experience of meeting you, they are more likely to remember you. Even if they can't remember you later, they will carry a positive association with you. That's a powerful thing to carry into a room with you when you meet them again under different circumstances. And when someone enjoys meeting you, they are more likely to ask for contact information or offer their business card. Wouldn't you rather have someone's number than an autograph? And when someone has a positive experience of meeting you, they are more likely to want to meet with you again and perhaps work with you. Tony Scott had a positive experience of meeting me. For about a hour, we never discussed my acting career until he said I might be Christa. Quentin and I had been talking for hours before an extremely well-timed fan recognized me and let him know I was an actor. I was a positive experience first and an actor second. If you have it within you to put others' egos in front of your own, you will find that it opens many doors.

Secondary Market Networking

If you live in Bismarck, North Dakota, you're less likely to run into people in the industry, but you can still network and increase "who you know." Maybe your state has a film commission or annual film festival. Some film commissions sponsor events and screenings the public is welcome to attend. Some have websites where you can post your resumé or learn the names of the local film commissioner and their staff. If your state has a film festival, attend. Many accept volunteers who get passes for films and events. Some festivals reach out to the public for script readers and people to screen the film submissions. Involving yourself in the local festival will not only put you in a position to meet the film organizers, you could also be put in a position to meet directors, producers and perhaps even studio executives.

No matter where you live, you can always mount your own project. By producing or directing, you will certainly meet actors and crew and you may find yourself meeting people throughout your local industry. When I was producing *Hell Ride*, I reached out to film commissions in California, New Mexico and Arizona. Just as when I produced my short films, I met with actors and crew. Making a movie is a collaborative experience and I was exposed to people and facilities that might be right for each of those projects. Before I moved to New Orleans, I made two trips to the city to prep a movie on which I was the writer, director and one of the producers. Though the financing fell through, in those two short visits, I met with the city and state film commissioners, the managers of two giant studio facilities, financiers, line producers, agents, casting directors, choreographers, and hotel marketing people. I toured dozens of locations, got headshots of local actors and ate the food of potential caterers. I even met with local shop owners and candy makers to discuss gift baskets. The trips were almost entirely tax deductible and many things were given to me for free in hopes that I would select a particular business or product. Though the movie ultimately fell through, I met dozens of local industry people. I learned who had good reputations, who the major players were and I found out a lot about how the industry works in Louisiana.

Many cities have script reading groups looking for actors to do their readings, acting groups or Facebook pages for local industry. Join what you can, participate when you can. Reach out to your community and widen the circle of "who you know."

Chapter 9:

Los Angeles

I can't tell you whether you should go to Los Angeles to pursue a career in acting. I can tell you that you can have a career in acting in other cities. But, if you do feel the need to go, here are some things I learned. In my experience, if you're moving to a larger market like Los Angeles, even if you're moving from New York with a good resumé, it takes about 2 years to settle in enough to really start working. If you're moving from a larger market to a smaller one, things can go much more quickly.

The City

Maybe you have a big stomach for traffic, but I didn't so I found it important to live in town in Los Angeles. The center of town for me was somewhere within a few miles of the intersection of Melrose and La Brea. I found peace living in the hills and some people love the beach. Much of my time was spent home alone so I tried to choose places that made me happy. The cost of living is very high in Los Angeles and, though it saves on commuting, finding a nice place to live near the center of town costs money. Some people like to spend money on cars, I spent mine on living in safe neighborhoods in places with character and less commuting time.

Los Angles has some beautiful areas and plenty of tourist attractions. Get to know the city, find places and activities that make you happy. There's step-climbing and pick-up volleyball at the beach. There are dog parks, some with long hiking trails and beautiful views. There are nightclubs, gyms, people-watching spots and plenty of movie theatres. Visit a museum, walk Hollywood Blvd. and look at the sidewalk stars, find a church. Make a life for yourself. Be interesting and well-rounded. Have experiences and meet people. You never know who you're talking to and anything can happen, but probably not in your living room.

The People

As I've said before, avoid spending too much time with "struggling actors." It's one thing to be out of work, it's quite another to be a victim of the industry.

Do the things you say you will do. It may shock you to find how unforgettable this can be. Unfortunately, lots of people are going to tell you they're going to call or meet you or come see your play and not do it. When I moved to L.A. in 1992, this was called "flaking" and it was totally acceptable. You can't control other people, but you can do the things you say you will and separate yourself from the crowd. Be a person of your word. It instills trust and trust can get you cast.

Los Angeles is a very seductive town. It runs on the fuel of dreams, but in much the same get-rich-quick way that Las Vegas does. Most of the dreamers suffer failure and rejection. Some rarely get anything else. But there is something heroic about the people who stop talking about going to L.A. and actually go. These dreamers follow a singleminded vision of what their life could be. Their dreams were so powerful, that the dreamers give up what they know, where they live and so much more to achieve their goals. The downside is that these dreamers aren't likely to pick your needs over their dreams. Relationships and friendships can be very tough in L.A. No one ever moved to L.A. to find their soulmate.

150

I have found that money, power and fame don't actually change a person so much as reveal them. Money, power and fame (just like alcohol) can lower inhibitions allowing someone the freedom to express their true desires. Perhaps you have friends who are doing well and behaving poorly. Maybe you're even worried you might change. As with alcohol, being rich and famous is like a permission slip. If you've been waiting all your life to pay back all the people who didn't believe in you, being rich and famous may afford you that opportunity. If you've always wanted to show off, you'll get your chance. If you've always wanted to give your old school a scholarship fund, you might be able to make that happen. You are you. Even when you're drunk and doing things you can't believe you did, you are you. If you've always dreamed of showing people you were better than them somehow, being rich and famous will give you the means to try. If you've always wanted to make the world a better place, being rich and famous will offer those opportunities too. Like alcohol, being rich and famous doesn't change a person, it reveals them. Money is not the root of all evil, it's the <u>love</u> of money. If you love people and enjoy your money, you and money will get along just fine. Fame doesn't make people assholes, it just shines a light on assholes and photographs them.

All of that said, go easy on your friends who are doing well and behaving poorly. New fame and money can be confusing for anyone. Remember before you learned your limits with alcohol? Sometimes it just goes to someone's head for awhile before they adjust. Even seasoned veterans struggle with things like getting awards. When I was starting out, I did a play in Hollywood and it was reviewed. I'd never been reviewed and didn't assume my name would be mentioned. After the play opened, the director brought in the newspapers and read them to the cast. The first review wasn't mean, but it wasn't nice. They used words like "clumsy" and "dull." The circle of actors looked so sad. Then, there it was, "Laura Cayouette is subtle and winning." Swept up in the surprise of it all, I squealed and clapped my hands. The next one was even tougher, using terms like "exaggerated bombast" and "painful" before calling my scene, "One of the best episodes." I was thrilled! Later, my dear friend and costar pulled me aside and said that she understood my excitement but not my timing. She pointed out that I was surrounded by people whose feelings had just been hurt, whose hard work had gone unrecognized or criticized. I've always been glad that she had the courage to confront me, that she had the patience to see my intentions were not bad and that the whole thing happened while I was still starting out. I never forgot that lesson and it has allowed me to be more compassionate when my good news hurts people close to me.

The "Day Job"

Find a job that lets you leave or that works nights and weekends. Ideally, you want a job where you are in charge of your own schedule. I had a job tutoring high school students for the S.A.T.'s. I was able to schedule the kids myself, all after 3 p.m. I had another job reading scripts for production companies. I would pick up a stack of scripts (this was before electronic versions) and be given a due date. I read them, evaluated them and wrote reports, all on my own schedule as long as I made the due date.

Some people make money bartending or waitressing. One friend bought an apartment building and rented out the units. I knew a dog walker and someone who made money selling things on eBay. Massage therapy is a popular job choice. In some cities, you can make a good living as a model. Try finding jobs that pay as much as possible in as few hours as possible.

In any case, the smartest thing to do is arrive with at least 6 months living expenses in savings. Perhaps this sounds impossible. Maybe you're convinced you'll be starring in your own show within 6 months. Almost everything takes longer than you think it will in the entertainment industry. I hope you do get lucky, but it's wise to be prepared. If you don't have what it takes to save up 6 months of money in order to pursue your goals, perhaps you don't have what it takes to survive the industry. No matter what happens, you certainly won't regret having money in the bank. I liked knowing that I could say "no." I turned down a few tempting parts that might surprise you and I'm so glad I did. Self-respect can be priceless and unforgettable.

Classes

If you're planning to take classes, start immediately. It will give your new life structure and exposure to new people. Ask around to find a good teacher and audit a number of different classes. As a general rule, if you're the best actor in the class, you're in the wrong class. It may be fun to hear how great you are every week, but your time and money are better spent being challenged by better actors.

The Lifestyle

Since you never know who you're talking to and anything can happen, especially in L.A., pretty much everything is an audition. I was once having a pretty irritating day so I decided to give myself the afternoon off (I'm not a completely unreasonable boss) and go to the movies. There were only about ten people in the theatre that sat over 300, and yet the guy sitting right behind me was one of the writer/producers of *Friends*. He said he loved working with me and talked about thinking of ways to bring my character back. Though it never happened, it was certainly an unexpected opportunity during what I thought of as time off.

Unexpected opportunities pop up a lot in Los Angeles. You never know who you might meet in a day and under what circumstances. It's wonderful in that it makes L.A. a target-rich environment for getting work. And it's terrible in that it means you may meet someone while you're nude in the steam room or because you just got in an argument with them in the grocery line. In L.A., everything's an audition because the only time you can be certain you aren't going to run into someone is in the sanctity of your own home. I guess that's why I always spent my money on rent and not on cars, though certainly many people find privacy in their cars.

The Warnings

When you're young, the urge to lose your virginity can seem overwhelming and yet lots of non-virgins will tell you, even warn you, that there's no rush. Moving to L.A. can be like that. People who've lived there won't tell you not to pursue your dreams, but they will caution you to be ready. They will worry that you will get hurt (and you probably will). They will caution you about their own bad experiences. They will caution you to "use protection." They will warn you about who to get involved with. They will enumerate obstacles and regrets. But, like curious virgins, you will hear none of it. You will probably be convinced that you are different, that it will go differently for you. You'll be convinced that you will get your "break" and that when you do, the town (the nation and the world!) will love you. That's fine. Maybe you will be different. Who knows? It happens and you may need that conviction to make such a bold move. But enjoy your anonymous years, the struggle that will turn into stories you tell on late night shows.

Be patient with the people who try to warn you off of moving. They are not crazy to worry for you. Like the non-virgins worrying for teenagers in a rush, they already know that taking that leap changes everything. You can't pop a cherry twice. You can't un-fuck yourself.

You find my language crass? Wait until you get to L.A. where cursing passes for conversation. L.A. is a tough town in so many ways. It's a huge city packed with millions of people where you can find yourself very alone. Money matters. Clothing matters. Haircuts and cars and looks matter. It's a lot to keep in perspective.

Why Go?

It is true that if you are trying to have a career in acting, you will probably have to go to Los Angeles at some point. The sheer quantity of work is enough reason to go. The infrastructure of agents, casting directors and teams of people whose entire job is to put actors to work is second to none. There are more studios there

154

than anywhere in the world. After I'd studied and done plays for almost 3 years in New York, I moved to L.A. because I thought I was ready to work and that's where the work was. We tend not to regret the things we did, but the things we never tried. If you feel the hunger to go, then don't let all of us nay-sayers scare you off of it. Fail forward if you must fail. But know that if it were easy, everyone would do it. Your odds of success are pretty darn bad. Your odds of struggling to keep up with the cost of living and being betrayed by someone who took advantage of your enthusiasm are pretty darn high. But, you have a right to insist on finding out for yourself why they were warning you. This is your one and only life. This is not the dress rehearsal. You only get one take. Make the most of it.

Chapter 10:

THE PEP TALK

The truth is that 95% of actors in the union make less than $5,000 a year, 4% make more but not enough to live on and 1% of all of the actors in the union make enough to live. I was unable to confirm these numbers through the union as they claim to collect no statistics on this, however, I read this in many books when I was starting out. In the past 20 years, union enrollment has gone up and wages now include bargain basement rates for everything from reality TV to commercials that play only on cable. In any case, the odds are heavily against you supporting yourself as an actor. That means that if you get a couple of national commercials and a recurring part on a TV show every year, you're in the same 1% as Tom Cruise and Emma Stone. I knew this before I ever started training. But many statistics haven't applied to me, so why should this one? I had been called to this profession and I was fearlessly answering the call. My mother always said, "Do what you love and the money will come." I loved writing, but from the moment I auditioned for entry into American Academy of Dramatic Arts and felt the power of genuinely affecting people, I knew I could find bliss in this calling and I never looked back. I fully committed.

Commitment

There's a scene near the end of *Indiana Jones and the Last Crusade* where Jones has to save his father from certain death. He follows a guide his father wrote to surmount obstacles and find the cup of the covenant. He trusts the guide book until the moment he comes to an infinitely deep chasm separating him from his goal. The guide indicates that Indiana must step into the abyss in order to reach the cup. He hesitates, but his need outweighs his fear and he raises his arms in surrender then lifts his leg and drops... onto a bridge that had been there all along. The chasm was an optical illusion. Several times in my career, I have stepped into the abyss and found the work was there all the time waiting for me to rise to the occasion of pursuing it.

When I say I fully committed, I mean that I: quit a great job managing a boutique and my dream job of teaching college; sold my house after only owning it for a year; got a room in New York, read as many books as I could find on the industry (history, biographies, breaking into the business, acting as a craft, acting as a career and more); studied at a conservatory for nearly 3 years; performed in off-off Broadway plays; auditioned for nearly one hundred commercials without booking anything; THEN moved to Los Angeles without ever having been there and without knowing anyone. Then I started all over again in L.A. More studying, more books, more plays, more auditions. Two more years went by and still, I never looked back. And then I started working. A little at first, then more and more. Work begets work.

I'm not saying that you have to quit your job and sell your house in order to work. I'm not even saying you have to go to New York or L.A. I love my new career in Louisiana. I never look back. But, if you want to be in the 1%, chances are you're going to have to give up a lot and find it within yourself to persevere when it feels like it's taking forever (especially if you've only put 2 years in and gone on 7 auditions). If you want this career, lots of things are going to feel like they're taking forever. I've waited over 3 months to hear whether I got the part–several times in my career. I've been told I didn't get the part and later been written into the movie as a different character–several times. There's an old saying that it takes 10 years to become an overnight success. If you don't believe it, check out the filmographies of people like Sharon Stone, Michelle Pfeiffer, George Clooney, Dennis Haysbert, Colin Firth, Tommy Lee Jones, Sir Ian McKellan, Jon Hamm, Samuel L. Jackson and Kathy Bates. Morgan Freeman began doing background work and under-5's at 27 years old. His big break came when he was cast in the children's series, *The Electric Company* at 40 years old. He was already 52 by the time *Driving Miss Daisy* came along and made him a household name. He probably would've been happy to <u>only</u> wait 10 years.

Find a healthy perspective on failure. For every person who wins an Oscar, there are four who make it to the wire and fail to win. I don't know about you, but if I ever get nominated for an Oscar, I seriously hope I don't see any part of it as a failure. For every person who gets a commercial, there are sometimes hundreds who fail to get the part. I heard 2,000 actors failed to get the Edward Norton part in *Primal Fear*. 4,000 little girls failed to get the part of "Hushpuppy" in *Beasts of the Southern Wild*. Think of that for a minute. At least 4,000 parents read lines with 4,000 girls between 6 and 8 years old. 4,000 little girls worked on their parts, suited up, showed up and were brave enough to do something scary while being judged by others. 4,000 little girls dared to fail. Would you call them failures because only one of them could get the part?

Make friends with failure. It is the downside of bravery and persistence, but it beats not trying. Failure can make us wiser, stronger and more experienced. The bottom line is that the higher you hope to climb, the more failure you will have to face and the more times you will have to find it within yourself to keep going.

Staying Motivated

I've been asked how to stay motivated without validation. The truth is that it's very hard. I have many tricks to combat it. When I was studying at the American Academy, they had framed class photos hanging on all the hallway walls and throughout the staircase.

Among them were class photos of Robert Redford, Lauren Bacall, Grace Kelly, Spencer Tracy and Gena Rowlands, but the one that I used as my inspiration was Danny DeVito. Everyday, as I'd walk up the stairs, I'd smile at his black and white image and think, "He must've heard a thousand times that he'd never make it in the industry. If someone who heard 'No' all the time could do this, certainly someone who'd never been told they wouldn't make it could do it." I owe him several debts of gratitude for all of his amazing work, but more so for the bravery he gave me, the audacity. I knew that I could dare to dream–I would just have to be amazing. If this career means anything to you, work hard to be amazing. Film is forever and you can shape your legacy.

Another trick I had was my "Wall of Inspiration." Some people use images or collages to remind them of why they are doing this. Many choose images of things they'd like to acquire, awards, property or goals they'd like to attain. I find that goals are very useful but I had a different idea for my wall when I moved to L.A. I started taping pictures of women who had the careers I wanted and women who'd paved the way for me, shown me that it can be done. There was Lucille Ball, who opened doors for smart, funny, tall redheads. There were actually quite a few tall girls in the mix: Julia Roberts, Laura Dern, Geena Davis and more. Then there were the ones who started late in life like I had; Ellen Barkin, Glenne Headly, Rene Russo (also tall). And those I hoped to be as good as one day: Shirley MacLaine, Vivien Leigh and Bette Davis. When I felt discouraged, I would look at those redheads, tall girls and late bloomers and know that they'd already pushed open the heavy doors of being the firsts. The task of following them would be easier. If they could take it when their task was so much more daunting, certainly I could persevere.

Know what you can control and what you cannot and focus your energy only on the things you can change. You cannot control whether you get the part, but you can show up prepared and on time. It's tempting to feel like a victim of circumstance, that it's your agent's fault you're not working or that you would've gotten the part if only your stupid ex hadn't texted you right before your audition.

Focus on being a pro and being amazing and don't let all the rejection and roadblocks get under your skin.

You can't change that this career is hard or unfair. You can accept that many careers are hard or unfair and your career choice involves multi-million dollar projects that can be seen globally in perpetuity. You can't change that you will fail many times. Just like buying lottery tickets, the more times you play, the more likely you are to lose. BUT, the more times you play, the better your odds of winning. Since we almost always lose, the best part of buying a lottery ticket is usually the time between the purchase and finding out whether you won. Those moments between are filled with imagining what you would do with the winnings and how winning might change your life. Those are the moments where we dare to believe it could all pay off. They are also opportunities to find out what you really care about, who you would be if money were no object. You can't change that only one person will get the part, but you can change your attitude about trying and failing. You can use those moments between to explore your values and imagine success. You can't change that this is a business and that people are counting on you to deliver. You can change how much time and energy you devote to being amazing.

Create Your Own Momentum

When people are playing jumprope and someone new wants to join in, they usually have to jump a few times to sync up with the pace of the rope before jumping in. Someone once told me that it takes three things happening to change your career. I thought they were going to tell me the three things, but that's not what they meant. They meant that it takes three boosts in your career to take you to the next level. Like with the jumprope, you have to sync up with the pace at the next level before you can jump in. When you're starting out, if you want to be at the level of getting an agent, you might need to get photos taken, join the union and get a good part in a good play. Later in your career, you may want to get the lead in a series. Perhaps the three boosts that will take you there will be getting an agent, doing several guest starring roles and redoing your reel. Still later, you may want to star in a specific big budget film. Perhaps the path will be to star in a movie, get the cover of People and meet the film's director.

I'm trying to make a few points, the largest being that the path is usually not; get agent, get discovered, become a star. If you wanted to become a professional basketball player, you would assume you'd have to be amazing, prepared, discovered and then be even more amazing. You'd assume that you'd have to dedicate yourself to the sport, mind and body and perhaps even soul. You wouldn't dare think, "Get basketball, get discovered, play for the NBA" without thinking you wouldn't have to work for it. If you want to do well in this business, even in a small way, you will have to work for it. You will have to dedicate your mind and body to the craft. But, when you have the opportunity to work, chances are that the "high" and its afterglow will keep you believing, at least for a moment, that you are doing something you were meant to be doing, something you're good at.

When I wanted to create momentum and there was nothing going on, I didn't call my agents and ask them why I wasn't going out. I didn't sit at coffee houses talking about how "slow" it was. I'd call my manager and we'd go to lunch. My manager, like many people you might know in a place like L.A., was able to get a table at pretty much any restaurant. We'd choose a restaurant where industry people would gather and "work the room." If she knew someone there, she'd introduce me as her client and try to turn the conversation into a meeting. If I knew someone, I'd introduce her and let her do her magic. If there was a premiere or screening of a movie that someone we knew had produced or directed, she would get us on the list and we'd dress up pretty. Maybe you don't have access to industry lunches or premieres, but you can find a film festival near you or form a support group.

Support

Yes, a support group. A friend of mine suggested, when we were both new to L.A., that we meet on Monday mornings and set goals, report achievements and troubleshoot problems. "The Support Ho's" was born. The Support Ho's met on Mondays for over 15 years. The faces changed, but the idea remained the same, that we would say things out loud and hold ourselves to them, that we would set goals and discuss progress and problems. There are many, many success stories and some amazing women sat at that table, including the 2-time Emmy winner (and 4-time nominee) Kathy Joosten.

If I ever doubted the power of saying things out loud and holding myself accountable, I would remember the time that, after not booking a commercial for what seemed like ages, I wrote down the goal and said out loud, "Book 3 commercials in 1 month." I created three momentum boosts including cutting my hair to half its length and getting new photos, but I did it. It really happened. After that, I never doubted the power of owning your goals. Dare to dream big, but know that the bigger the dream, the larger the commitment. Forming and maintaining a support group takes energy and commitment. Even just attending a support group, class or theatre company takes energy and commitment. You tend to get out of things what you're willing to put into them. You can't control whether you get the part, but you can create an environment that is encouraging and forces you to declare your goals.

Another trick is to go where the love is. Getting rejections all over town? Try doing a student film or a play or some other free work. I've had the privilege of directing Richard Dreyfuss, Mircea Monroe, Joanna Cassidy, Julie Brown and Danica McKellar, all for free. If they can work for free, so can you. Work begets work. Even free work can lead to work. If you're any good at all, chances are people will be grateful that you contributed to their no-pay project. After a long day of hearing that you didn't get any paying gigs, it can be very inspiring and reinvigorating to go to a set where people are grateful for your contributions. If a director or producer said they wanted to work with you on a future project, keep tabs on their career and send then postcards or emails letting them know what you're up to, especially if you're creating momentum. They already like you so you've already crossed that hurdle. You're going where you're valued.

When the only casting director calling me for commercial auditions kept having to request me, I went to him for clarification. My agency was showing me no love but he kept calling me in so I went where the love was to course correct. Maybe you're like the Sally Field character in *Soapdish* and it's just been too long since someone reminded you that you're great. Go visit the high school drama coach who inspired you or call the friend who drove cross-country with you. Plug back into the people and things that inspired you and refuel.

Watch Movies and Television

And, for goodness sake, watch movies and television. Watch the movies that you loved as a kid, the ones that made you want to be an actor, the ones you always meant to see, the ones that changed acting forever. When Marlon Brando picked up Eva Marie Saint's dropped glove then tried to pull it over his meaty hand in *On the Waterfront*, the "Method" was illustrated so perfectly that simply acting would never be enough again. His choices created a reality so alive and in the moment that it was unignorable. Watch movies and TV because they have something to teach you about the heritage of your craft. Watch them because a great movie can inspire you and remind you why you started doing this in the first place. Watch them because movies and TV are filled with unforgettable moments.

Doubt

Fight fear with love. When you find yourself doubting, dive into the things that inspire you and let them work their magic on you. If you love acting, then act. Find a play or a student film and just act. If you have to, set up a camera and record yourself doing monologues. Do what you love. If you love playing golf, nine holes might give you a better attitude. Maybe your love is yoga or fishing or going to the movies. Whatever it is, taking time to do what you love can make you brave in the face of fear. At the very least, it can offer you an escape and some time to refuel.

How do you know if you're just being impatient or if it's over? Most of us could find it in ourselves to hang in there if we knew for sure that it was all going to work out. Faith is about believing in things you can't see. But, going too long without validation can make even the most tenacious lose the faith. I once asked Richard Dreyfuss about this, about being afraid that maybe I was crazy to try this or not good enough. He asked how often I felt this way.

"Every few months or so, a few times a year."

He laughed, "That's nothing, you're fine."

It helped knowing that everyone has doubts. He then confessed that he went 3 years without a job. That must have been terrifying to live through. After the first couple of years, the last 6 months must have been agony. His career got a second wind with *Down and Out in Beverly Hills* and he went on to be nominated for still more awards including Academy Award and Golden Globe nominations for *Mr. Holland's Opus*.

I can't tell which of your jobs is your last. I don't know if it's over for you. What I do know is that it's normal to doubt and everyone battles it at some point. Some people have what I call "Impostor's Complex." The more successful and/or famous they become, the more they worry that they will be found out, that we will all discover that they weren't really that good after all. I've never experienced that type of anxiety but I think it's because I really prepared myself as an actor before I tried to get work. There were times I was intimidated sitting next to someone with a fold-out resumé and a face I recognized, but I knew there was a chance I might be the best choice for the part. Perhaps if this fear is dogging you, then taking classes, hiring a coach and becoming a better, more prepared actor might help you to feel less like an impostor.

I can't always be prepared for every audition. Sometimes I've only had the sides for a few minutes. Sometimes I've had too many auditions in one day, all with full scripts I had to read and pages and pages of sides and even wardrobe changes. When you know you're not really ready to dazzle the Bigwigs with your acting abilities, just make strong choices and be good in the room.

Has anyone ever quoted you back to yourself or to other people? Has anyone ever remembered something you said, something they found unforgettable, something that you don't even remember saying? Do people you don't recognize remember meeting you? Do they remember details about you, where you're from or that you have two sisters? If so, you are probably at least a little bit unforgettable. Ivana Chubbuck made herself unforgettable by not talking about herself at a party. Some people have an unforgettable physical trait–wild curly hair or a memorable tattoo. I wish I had unforgettably cured cancer or ended world hunger, but I'm happy with being unforgettable in projects I can be proud of. And I've never wanted to be famous for being famous. The point is that being unforgettable is the goal, not getting the part. It's okay to doubt you'll book a job, but it's not okay to let doubt make you blow a moment.

If you know you can't blow the Bigwigs away with your reading, be great in the room. Be professional and don't forget to have fun. If you can't guarantee an unforgettable performance, just be your naturally unforgettable self. Never forget that you might be the one who looks like "the one," the one they'll give a second chance just because of your look or personality. When you focus on getting the part, you give your power away to the Bigwigs casting the jobs. When you focus on the fact that you didn't have enough time to prepare, you give away your power. You have so little power in the situation to begin with, you can't afford to give any of it away. Push doubt aside and focus on being amazing. Focus on having a unique take and being prepared for anything. Focus on the opportunity, not the outcome.

The Fish that Got Away

Every actor has a story of the "big fish that got away". The big fish is the part that can change your career's trajectory. It's the starring role that could put you on the cover of People Magazine, get you the best tables at restaurants, open velvet ropes at clubs and get you into some big agency.

Is it tougher to go on over 100 auditions without getting any work, or is it harder to survive getting down to the wire on a part that could change your life? I'll be honest with you, they both suck and they both gnaw at your confidence. The Lesson of the 100 Auditions got me through those times of not getting work and I hope it lends you a new perspective to get through that kind of frustration and fear. The big fish moment is different because, rather than feeling like a failure during most of the journey then finally getting a job, the fish that got away fills you with hope all along the way then deals the crushing blow that you're not getting the part.

My big fish came my way because a casting director believed in me and was excited about my potential. Though she'd been told not to bring in any "unknowns," she staked her reputation on her hunch about me and put me on tape. I prepared myself silly and hired Ivana Chubbuck to coach me. The part was the female lead across one of the biggest stars in the world at that time. It was a smaller part and the male lead could be counted on to bring in the money so I believed I had a shot. The casting director and her associate explained that they would allow me to do as many takes as I needed so not to feel any pressure. They assured me that they wanted to help me to get a great take and they were willing to stay all night.

The scene was essentially a 8 to 10 minute argument. Knowing that it could come off as negative and no fun, I made choices I hoped would be entertaining and keep my partner engaged in keeping the argument going. When I was done with the first take, I looked to the casting directors faces. Both of them stood dumbfounded with their mouths open. They looked at each other then at me then said, "I think we got it." They let me know that they would make a point of the fact that I was the only actress to use her first and only take. I left there on a cloud pulled over a rainbow by unicorns. But, I knew the odds were pretty bad for me against all those "name" actresses so I tried to put it out of my mind.

Quite some time later, I got a call from my manager saying that the movie had a "short list" for the part and that I was on it! I knew that the odds were still awful, but things were definitely going my way so far. To celebrate without getting carried away, I came up with a rule. I allowed myself to spend 5 minutes a day thinking about what it would be like if I got the part.

Then things got even crazier. I was away working with someone who I knew was also on the list when I got another call from my manager. They had thrown out that list and there was a new list with only four names on it. Miraculously enough, my name was the only one that had made it to the next list. But, the caliber of women I was competing with was now even higher. I was up against some of the heaviest hitters and biggest names in the industry. I rewarded myself with 15 minutes a day of daydreaming about my new future.

As you already know, the next call was probably the hardest one my manager ever had to make. Certainly, she had allowed herself to dream how her career might change as well. It was a sad day for both of us. A very sad day. I decided to throw myself a "pity party." I invited two very supportive friends, including Jernard Burks, to spend the evening with me and help me through. After I told my big fish story, Jernard came up with a genius rule for the pity party. For 15 minutes out of every hour, we would focus on how much this sucked. For the other 45, we'd focus on fun things including how amazing it was that I almost got that part. Jernard pointed out that the woman who beat me had been acting her whole life and that she was the one of the most heavily awarded actors of all time. He reminded me that I had come to this career late and was a nobody and yet I gave her a run for the money. I would have to be pretty darn talented to do that and I would be just as talented at my next audition.

To this day, it's one of the best auditions of my career. It still hurts to watch my audition scene in the movie. There's no place on your resumé for big fish stories so I get no credit for almost getting the part. I even debated telling this story in this book because I have nothing to show for it. I wasn't even offered a smaller part. There's no happy ending. I decided to tell the story because it is hard to get so close and come away empty-handed. Just like you will need to be strong when nothing's going your way, you will have to be strong when it looks like everything might. You will have to dig deep to get past losing out when it was all within reach. Find a way to be proud of yourself and give yourself credit for competing so well with the best. And I told the story because I wanted to share the joy of a good pity party done well.

Why Do It

I can't tell you if you'll become one of the 1%. I don't know if you should sell your house and move to L.A. What I do know is that this career has been immensely rewarding. I've traveled the world and met movie stars, captains of industry, politicians and Pope John Paul II. I've worked with so many Academy Award winners and nominees that I've lost count. I've been directed by Tony Scott, Sam Raimi and Quentin Tarantino–twice. I've directed Richard Dreyfuss saying my lines to me. I've attended Cannes, the Golden Globes and the People's Choice Awards as well as countless other award shows and premieres and even went to a party at the Playboy Mansion. For years, I was on TV somehow everyday and was part of the *Friends*, *Nash Bridges and The Larry Sanders Show* era. I've watched myself in foreign countries with some other actress saying my lines in French or Italian. Now I'm a comic book character. It's been an amazing journey.

The cost has been high. My dream was to write novels and teach college. Now I'm more likely to play a teacher or novelist in a movie. I missed my grandmother's funeral because I was cast in my second TV show, *Flipper*, in Australia and had to choose. I've missed weddings and births, vacations and reunions, holidays and birthdays. Was it worth it? My father made choices about his career that cost him time with us and moments with us, but I doubt he ever questioned his career choice. I chose my career a lot. I still choose my career a lot. It's what I do for a living, it's how I get my insurance, it's where my pension is. It's important.

There are times when this career can feel humiliating. Sometimes it's a blessing to miss the occasional wedding or reunion and avoid having to answer the question, "What have I seen you in?" if you haven't been working. You may have starred in a TV show that ran successfully for eight seasons then not be able to get work anymore because everyone identifies you with that character. You may tell everyone to watch a movie only to discover you were cut. I was once hired for a part because I fit the dress. I'm not kidding. I didn't even meet the director until I was on set. I reminded myself that it didn't matter if the Bigwigs thought they had basically hired an animated mannequin, it was an opportunity to turn a minute into a moment. It's not actually humiliating to get a job because of your measurements, it's just humbling. It's not actually humiliating to have a credit that reads,"Party Guest #1," it's just humbling. Get over yourself and get back to making the most of your moments.

The Gift of Acting

There are parts of me that cannot be changed. I'm tall, slight and fair. There are certain parts I will never get just because of my height, age or coloring. I had my Wall of Inspiration to remind me I wouldn't be the first tall girl or redhead, but what really kept me going was something Richard Dreyfuss once said to me, "The very things that keep them from hiring you in the beginning will be the very things they can't live without when you make your mark." I thought of Danny DeVito, how his stature and gruff exterior must have held him back from many parts he would've killed. Now, he's a "type" and if you want that type, he's the only one. He made himself essential.

I can't promise you that you don't need to consider dental work or a name change (Arnold Schwarzenegger???), but I can tell you that over 6 foot tall Geena Davis found work as a quirky girl in small parts like the underwear-clad soap star in *Tootsie*, then became an essential leading lady in the '90s. Jonah Hill is now a type. Heck, even muscle-bound Arnold Schwarzenegger became a type and one of the biggest stars in the history of cinema.

Some people are motivated to pursue an acting career in hopes of gaining riches and fame. The truth is that most of us, even the ones with dreams of riches and fame, just really love acting–even when we don't get paid and no one sees the work. Pursuing a career in acting may be a lot like running away and joining the circus, but it can also be a noble profession. My mother used to be a therapist and when I started my career, she told me that her patients used movies as "emotional shorthand." They would say things like, "You know the scene in (a movie) where the (character) does (such and such), it was just like that." Movies and television shows and even commercials help us to connect to ourselves outside of ourselves. People all over the country work in offices and recognize all the players in *The Office* or *Office Space*. They get a chance to laugh at the absurdity of their own lives. They get to laugh at themselves. Movies often have bad guys who hurt people the way we've been hurt, then we get to see them blown up or humiliated in front of their peers. The nerd can get the girl. The underdog can prevail. The regular guy can be bit by a spider and become a superhero. Scrappy people can survive against all odds. History can be relived or even reimagined. The future is what you make of it.

It is a privilege to be part of America's #1 export– entertainment. Actors are given the opportunity to illuminate, illustrate and educate. For many of us, acting is a calling. After 20 years of playing other people, I have gotten to walk a mile in many people's shoes. For me, this is the gift of acting. The gift it gives viewers is the opportunity to "meet" someone you invented in order to best tell the story. The gift it can give the actor is an opportunity to explore compassion. In order to best play Hitler, you must find the part of you that sees how he came to be a mass murderer and how he justified his actions. You must find his righteousness. To play an adulterer, you must find the part of you willing to run wrecking balls through people's lives to follow your passion. Acting can lead you down a path of learning to love people for the complicated messes they are and that is truly a gift.

Believe

When I was starting out, I believed to my core that I was supposed to be an actor. I read a book called *Creative Visualization* that talked about the power of thought, the energy of belief. The more recent version of this would be *The Secret*. It's easy to believe you won't work when the odds are stacked against you. It takes faith to believe you will work, faith that you are doing what you're supposed to be doing.

It's very hard to make anything happen without first being able to see it and believe it's possible. Visualize yourself working. Picture yourself doing well at auditions, making strong connections, getting bigger and better parts. See yourself on set, sitting in your cast chair with your character's name on it. Picture yourself on the red carpet, accepting an award, getting your star on the Walk of Fame. It's normal to worry but worrying is focusing on what you don't want. Many people are totally prepared for things not working out but find themselves unprepared for success.

Even the losers get lucky sometimes and if you prepare hard enough, go where the love is and be unforgettable, anything can happen. Anything. If you don't believe in your ability to work, why should anyone else? Invest in yourself and your career. Dare to fail. I'd rather fail trying than wonder what might have been. Those are your options–risk failure or quit. For every person that gets the job, there can be hundreds who tried and thousands who envy you the opportunity to risk failure. Not every person will work, but there is work for every type of person. Rejection is hard but failure is a matter of perspective. I try to fail forward. I'd rather fall on my face than sit on my ass. I have believed from the start that there was work for me in this industry. I believe in my ability to rise to the occasion of my career and meet my opportunities with preparation. Even after over 100 failed attempts at booking a commercial or years without representation, I always believed I would work.

I love movies and TV. After a period of feeling stuck and not working for months, I realized that my approach was all wrong. Rather than focusing on what this industry could do for me, I started focusing on what I could <u>contribute</u> to the history of film and television. I started working again almost immediately. I cherish the many magical journeys actors have taken me through in movies and TV. I'm grateful for all the actors who touched my soul, revealed inner truths and made me laugh, cry, gasp or scream. I believe in the power of acting. I believe in the importance of entertainment. I believe I have something to contribute and a responsibility to try. Believing in yourself may not pay the rent, but if you believe you have something to contribute, you can find the strength to try again. The alternative is quitting. Acting is not for everyone and there are plenty of very good reasons to quit. For me, quitting never really entered my brain. In this book, there's a chapter on waiting and another on failure, but there is no chapter on quitting. If you need to quit, you don't need a chapter to do that and I'm no authority on how to survive it. I suspect that, if you're still reading this, you love acting and can't wait to do it again. So, believe. Believe enough to commit and want it enough to stay motivated to do what it takes. Believe because it's better to believe and be wrong than to not even try. Believe because it will keep you going. Believe because you might be right. If you're right about this life being for you, amazing experiences await.

This Is Not the Dress Rehearsal

Auditions are opportunities, but they are also like lottery tickets. The more times you play, the better your chances of hitting the jackpot. When you hit a year-long dry spell or you're just starting out, remember that if you knew the next job was only 12 more auditions away, you might be pretty glad to be losing that 11th one. Your career is only truly important to you. You alone are responsible for your choices and your dedication. As I said before, this is your one and only life. This is not the dress rehearsal. You only get one take. Make the most of it.

Maybe my career doesn't look like what I though it might when I was studying Shakespeare and Ibsen in New York, but I've created a niche for myself carving out small parts and turning them into moments. And because I never quit, perhaps the best is yet to come. If you want to be a star, I wish you well, but I've had an amazing adventure and made a modest but decent living doing what I love without ever being famous. Either way, if you work in this industry, you will play small parts and each part is an opportunity to turn minutes into moments and moments into a career.

Glossary

2-shot - a shot of you and one other person

actor's reel - a compilation of clips from your career

background actors - actors with no lines

backstory - the personal and professional history of a character

base camp - where the trailers are located, usually close to the set

Bigwigs - for the purposes of this book - directors, producer, studio executive and casting directors

breakdown - a description of the character and their place in the plot

buyout - a commercial where they pay you a one time fee and no residuals

close-up - a shot that features your face

cover, coverage - shooting a scene from several directions

"day job" - the job you pay the bills with while pursuing your career

dipping - Margie Haber technique of moving your eyes down to pick up the rest of the sentence on your sides

first team - principal actors, actors with lines

"going up" on a line - forgetting your next line

"hip pocket" - when an agency sends you out without signing you

"in the can" - coming from the days of putting film in cans after it was shot; it means the shot is completed to everyone's satisfaction

insert shots - shots of some detail including hands, wardrobe, props and products

looping - recording the dialogue after a movie is shot

marks - tape, sandbags or tiny dot stickers, etc. placed where your feet should be

master shot - a shot that includes everyone in the scene

Method acting - an approach to acting developed by Constantin Stanislavski, Lee Strasberg and members of the Group Theatre where the actor uses their own memories and experiences to enrich a character

minis - the call sheet and the pages from the script that will be shot that day all shrunken down to about 5x8

moment before - the moment before the scene began

"moving on" - when the director and the stars are happy with the take and ready to start the next

"nice casual" - most common wardrobe description which can mean different things for different types and age ranges but the general idea is to look put together in a non-distracting way

objective - what you want in the scene

off-book - memorized

period piece - a project set in another era

"playing the ending" - anticipating, indicating, forgetting to stay in the moment

"plus one" - a guest to an invitation-only event or party

principle actor - an actor with a credit

residuals - money owed you every time a film, TV show or commercial runs on TV or is sold as a DVD

SAG-AFTRA - the actors' union (Screen Actors Guild–American Federation of Television and Radio Arts)

secondary markets - states outside of California that have up-and-running film industries

sides - the script pages being used for an audition

slate - your filmed introduction at an audition featuring your name, profiles and sometimes your agency, height, special skills

stand-in - someone whose job is to look like you and stand in your spot for lighting and camera set-ups

storyboards - the story of the commercial drawn out like a comic strip of the shots

"struggling actors" - actors who complain more than they work

type - a category of actors usually defined by physical appearance including age, height, weight and general "look"

typecast - playing the same part over and over

unique take - making choices about the scene and the character that only you could make based on your own history and perspective

working actors - actors who make a living acting

List of Movies

This is a comprehensive list of all the films mentioned in *Know Small Parts*. I've left out TV shows, TV movies, plays, short films and books mentioned in the book. Most of the movies listed are truly great and I recommend you make a point of seeing them. That said, some are listed because I mentioned them in reference to actors being cast in small parts or cut from the film, not because they were must-see movies.

Accepted
The Accused
All About Eve
Almost Famous
American Graffiti
The Asphalt Jungle
Badlands
Beasts of the Southern Wild
The Big Chill
Blue Sky
Bob Roberts
Boogie Nights
Boyz n the Hood
Bulworth
Can't Hardly Wait
Castaway
The Color Purple
Constantine
The Contender
Dangerous Minds
Dangerous Years
The Dark Knight
Dazed and Confused
Dead Man Walking
Death Proof
Detroit Rock City
Django Unchained
Down and Out in Beverly Hills
Driving Miss Daisy
E.T.: The Extra-Terrestrial
Encino Man
Enemy of the State

Erin Brockovich
Escape from New York
The Evening Star
Fandango
Fast Times at Ridgemont High
First Wives Club
For Love of the Game
Frances
From Dusk Till Dawn
Full House
Galaxy Quest
Gentlemen Prefer Blondes
Ghost World
Glengarry Glen Ross
The Godfather
Gone with the Wind
Gosford Park
The Graduate
Grease
Green Grass of Wyoming
Hairspray
Harold and Kumar Go to White Castle
To Have and Have Not
Hell Ride
Hot Fuzz
The House Bunny
How to Marry a Millionaire
I Am Legend
I Am Sam
Indiana Jones and the Last Crusade
Interview with the Vampire
Irma la Douce
Jungle Fever
Kill Bill: Vol. 1 & 2
Krippendorf's Tribe
La Bamba
The Lake House
Lethal Weapon
Logan's Run
Look Who's Talking
Man in the Moon

The Matrix
Meeting Daddy
Men Don't Leave
Milk
Misery
Money Talks
Mr. Holland's Opus
My Big Fat Greek Wedding
Never Back Down 2: The Beatdown
Office Space
On the Waterfront
Planet Terror
The Player
Postcards From the Edge
Precious
Pretty Woman
Primal Fear
The Prime of Miss Jean Brodie
Private Benjamin
Pulp Fiction
Radio Flyers
Raiders of the Lost Ark
Ray
Reservoir Dogs
The Rocky Horror Picture Show
Saturday Night Fever
Scream
Scudda Hoo! Scudda Hey!
The Shocking Miss Pilgrim
Shawshank Redemption
Silverado
Soapdish
Steel Magnolias
A Streetcar Named Desire
Swingers
Superbad
Taxi Driver
Terminator 2: Judgement Day
Terms of Endearment
Thelma and Louise
Thin Red Lin

Made in the USA
San Bernardino, CA
27 August 2018